The Unforgettable Story of a Man
Who Discovered the Adventure of

THE CALLING

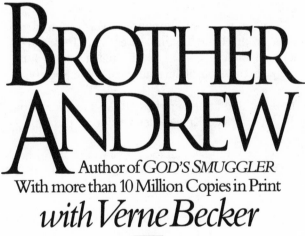

BROTHER ANDREW

Author of *GOD'S SMUGGLER*
With more than 10 Million Copies in Print

with Verne Becker

MOORINGS
NASHVILLE, TENNESSEE

A DIVISION OF THE BALLANTINE PUBLISHING GROUP
RANDOM HOUSE, INC.

THE CALLING

Published in association with Sealy M. Yates, Literary Agent,
Orange, California.

Library of Congress Catalog Card Number: 95-81695

First Edition: February 1996
10 9 8 7 6 5 4 3 2 1

Printed in the United States of America

Contents

Introduction

Many years ago while traveling in Eastern Europe, I spoke in an evangelical church in East Germany. I forgot what I preached on, but I never forgot what the pastor did as I finished my message. He came up on the platform, put his arms around me, and began to cry.

As he regained his composure, he began to tell us all the story of Joseph in Genesis 37. Joseph was home and his brothers were out tending the flocks of sheep and cattle. Joseph's father, Jacob, sent him to find out where they were and how they were faring. While Joseph wandered around the fields, a man stopped and asked him, "What are you seeking?"

Joseph answered, "I am seeking my brothers."

When the pastor, with his arm still around my shoulder, reached that point in the story, he broke down in tears again. "This is what Brother Andrew is doing!" he exclaimed. "He is seeking his brothers."

Today I am still seeking my brothers and sisters around the world who are suffering for their faith—not only because they need me, but because I need them. We are all part of the same fellowship of believers, which the Bible calls the body of Christ. We need one another. We all have a calling to do God's work—together.

◄○►

The political, social, and spiritual landscape of the earth has shifted dramatically since I first visited the communist world in 1955. Little did I know that my life would be turned upside down as a result of that visit, and that I would later become known as "God's Smuggler"—the title of my first book. In the meantime, the ministry of Open Doors has grown from a box of Bibles and a Volkswagen to an international organization operating in more than a hundred countries. Though we devoted a large part of our effort to serving the church in Eastern Europe and the Soviet Union, my heart was also broken by the persecution of Christians in other parts of the world, such as Communist China, Marxist Latin America, turbulent Africa, and the Muslim-dominated areas. So, in much the same way that I traveled behind the Iron Curtain, I "sought my brothers" in those countries, too, and helped organize ministry teams to support and encourage the suffering church there.

Now that the Berlin Wall has toppled, the Cold War has ended, and the Soviet Empire has crumbled, we rejoice in the newfound freedom of Christians in these countries to worship God and share the good news of Christ openly. But we must not stop praying for and supporting these brothers and sisters because they are facing a host of new challenges: deteriorating economies, political instability, and the moral temptations that accompany such freedoms. And they still struggle with a severe shortage of Bibles and Christian literature. If anything, they need more prayer and assistance, not less.

From the very start, however, my vision—and that of Open Doors—has been to reach the persecuted church in "closed" countries. So with the official opening of the Soviet bloc, we have been shifting more of our resources to other areas where the church suffers at the hands of repressive governments, especially in the Muslim world.

Even though Islam may be the world's fastest growing religion, a very small percentage of Christian missions activity is directed to the Islamic world. Many Christians write off the Muslim world as closed to the Christian faith. And yet a small but struggling church there desperately needs our prayers and our help. As I will soon explain, the message of Christ is spreading there in remarkable ways. But with that advancement comes incredible obstacles. That is why I've made it a priority to bring the good news of Jesus Christ into these areas, just as I did into the Iron Curtain countries. The locations may change, but our mission is still the same: "Wake up! Strengthen what remains and is about to die" (Revelation 3:2).

◄○►

In my first book, *God's Smuggler,* many of you read the amazing stories of believers I met in Russia and in Eastern Europe. Now you will have the chance to meet brothers and sisters from other parts of the world as well. Because many of these saints are in constant danger of arrest, imprisonment, or death because of their faith in Jesus, I will disguise some of the details of their situations in order to protect their identities. But the authentic power of their faith and commitment cannot be disguised.

For years people have asked me, "Andrew, how do you get in to so many forbidden countries? How do you meet all these important people whom you can influence for the Lord? And why are you still active rather than locked up in some prison cell?"

I'm going to let you in on a little secret. I am by no means an extraordinary person or even a particularly gifted person. I never went to high school or college. All I had was two years of training at a missionary school. I tell people that I'm a dumb Dutchman, the son of a blacksmith, and that I work for a Jewish carpenter. In other words, I'm just an ordinary guy who has tried to listen for God's calling in my life and then obey.

Reflecting over the past forty years of my ministry, however, I have been able to recognize a process by which God has worked in my life and brought about the small contributions I've made to advancing the kingdom of God. Further, I have come to realize that this progressive work of God is not at all unique to me, but is something he wants to bring about in the life of every Christian.

So in addition to giving you a firsthand, up-to-date chronicle of my more recent encounters with the suffering, triumphant church, I want to share that process with you in this book. I have broken it down into ten steps, which will be scattered throughout the narrative to encourage you to pause from time to time and focus on your personal responsibility as part of the worldwide body of Christ. (At the end of the book, I have included an outline of all ten steps and their accompanying prayers to help you use them in your own life.)

These steps describe what can happen when you pay attention to the call of God in your everyday lives—in your homes, your schools, your neighborhoods, your workplaces—and then follow it. Because it is here that we can begin changing the world. Our faith in Christ must become a way of life, wherever we are.

When that happens, it won't be long before you begin to see the entire world, and your part in it, with different eyes. You will discover that God is opening doors for you to serve him in ways you never thought were possible.

Brother Andrew

Chapter One

◄O►

From the Inside Out

*I*t was August 1968, and I was working in my office when my kids yelled up the stairs to me.

"Daddy!" they said. "There's something terrible on TV!"

Astonished, I jumped up from my desk and ran downstairs. At that time no Dutch stations broadcasted midday, so I knew that if anything at all was on TV, it was probably serious.

On the screen I saw row upon row of tanks rolling across Czechoslovakia toward the capital city of Prague, along with transport vehicles carrying thousands of troops. The Russian army had just invaded the country. The TV cameras panned the faces of a bewildered population, most of them gazing in stunned silence, a few of them reacting in anger at the Russian presence.

As I watched the news coverage, I wondered: *How would this affect my friends in the church there? They might be crushed by the Russians. What do they need? How can I help?* So I quickly loaded my big Citroen station wagon with Russian Bibles and Christian booklets in Czech, and I headed straight for the Czech border. Because there were no speed limits in most of Europe, I drove around one hundred miles per hour and made it in only a day.

At the border crossing, I could hardly believe the sight. Facing me was a line of cars stretching as far down the road as I could see. Thousands of Czech citizens were anxiously trying to leave the country, fleeing before the advancing Russian army.

Meanwhile, mine was the only car going in.

The border guards were overwhelmed. A uniformed soldier came over and leaned into my window. The barrel of the machine gun slung over his shoulder pointed dangerously close to my head.

"Do you know what is happening in my country?" he said. His face looked sad, defeated.

"Yes," I said, "I know all about it."

"And you still want to go in?"

"That is the very reason I want to go in, sir."

He shrugged his shoulders, stamped my passport—I didn't even have a visa—and waved me through. He was too busy helping people get out. Never mind a fool who wanted to get in. Well, in I went. Amid all the confusion nobody bothered to check my luggage. I hadn't even hidden my boxes of Bibles.

The Czech citizens in the line of cars waiting to leave the country gave me strange looks as I passed them. Only a few miles beyond the end of that line I was stopped by the Russian army. The fields on both sides of the road had been turned into huge camps, teeming with tanks and trucks and troops and artillery. And on that narrow road two huge green tanks blocked the way and pointed their cannons right at my station wagon, which suddenly seemed very tiny.

At times like these you have no time for a prayer meeting. You rely on the faith and prayers of your partners back home and on the words of Jesus. As several uniformed soldiers with machine guns approached, I barely had time to say my little smuggler's prayer: "Lord Jesus, I have Scriptures I want to take to your children in this land. When you were on earth, you made so many blind eyes to see. Now I ask you to make these seeing eyes blind."

The soldier abruptly held out his hand for my passport. As he checked it over, I thought he had it upside down, but I figured he couldn't read it anyway. A second later he handed it back without a word and allowed me to pass.

I finally pulled into Prague, which was swarming with columns of tanks and Russian troops. The huge tanks clattered and clanged on the cobblestones, tearing up many of the roads and terrifying the local residents. Upon seeing the foreign license plates of my car, the people would raise their arms in welcome, which made me nervous because it drew attention to me. I'd look in my rearview mirror at the tank looming behind, and worry that it would simply roll right over me as if I were an empty Coke can.

On the first Sunday of the occupation, I preached in the same church that I mention in my book, *God's Smuggler*. I even had the same interpreter, Antonin. In spite of the rumbling of tanks and the sporadic crackling of gunfire in the streets, the church was packed. The people had come because they were wondering why this had happened to them. I first brought them greetings from Christians in the West, and I assured them that our prayers were with them in this new time of hardship. They would not be forgotten. But then, amid the rattling of windows, I went on to explain why I felt the crackdown had occurred.

"If we do not go to the heathen with the gospel," I stressed in my message, "they will come to us as revolutionaries and occupation armies." It was a theme I would emphasize for the next three decades.

They quickly realized I was speaking about the church's missed opportunity to reach the Russians. During the past nine months the Czech people had enjoyed a reasonable amount of freedom under Alexander Dubcek. But the Christians, rather than seizing the occasion to go to Russia with Bibles and preachers, went instead to the West to buy new dresses, shoes, bicycles, tape recorders, radios, even cars. They were taken in by the materialism of the West. And they forgot their big brother to the East. Now the Russians had suddenly clamped down, and gone was their liberty. It was not an easy thing to tell them, but it had to be said.

A sense of remorse swept over the congregation. "What would happen now?" the people wondered aloud. Would God turn against them?

"No!" I said. "God loves you, and he also loves the Russians. Since you didn't go to the Russians with Bibles, God in his infinite love allowed the Russians to come to you. Now you have the opportunity to give them the Word of God." It was a new idea to many of them, and it brought tears to their eyes.

After the service they came up to me and said, "Andrew, if only we had known. If only we were prepared for the Russian occupation. But we have no Russian Bibles. How can we help them?"

"Now, why do you think I came?" I answered with a smile. And I began to unpack my load of Russian Bibles and hand them out to people as they left the church. Elated, they divided them up and took to the streets, offering them to the Russian troops throughout the city.

Keep in mind that the young soldiers were scared. They had been told that they would be welcomed by the Czechs, but instead people were spitting at them, shaking their fists, shouting, cursing, throwing rocks, and heaving Molotov cocktails. Street signs had been turned around or removed or painted over to confuse them, and they could not even get a drink of water from the Czechs. But then all of a sudden the Christians came walking up to them with big smiles on their faces and said, "God bless you. God is love and God loves you. Here is a Bible. Won't you accept the love of God and read how God loves you?" Soon we had other teams doing the same thing in other Czech cities. They went to the Russians with the love of God and with the Book of God.

And something amazing happened—something we can never fully explain: I later received reports from several cities that within ten days, the Soviet leaders had to recall and replace the entire Russian occupation army! They had become completely demoralized. I have to believe that the love and the Bibles shared by Christians played some part in their withdrawal. After all, the Bible, the Word of God, changes people. And changed people change the situations around them.

—◄o►—

One day in 1961 I was driving my blue Volkswagen across Holland and West Germany on my way to a Bible conference in East Germany. This was a critical time in the Cold War. Tensions were running especially high over the presence of Soviet missiles in Cuba. High anxiety prevailed throughout the world as the threat of nuclear war loomed. Christians in East Germany were still operating quite freely, due in large part to the deaconess movement in the East German church. Like a Protestant order of nuns, the deaconesses carried on much of the evangelism, Bible instruction, and social service in the country. They showed Christ's love by caring for people the system had no use for.

Many of the deaconesses worked as nurses in hospitals, and they would often sing hymns and pray with their patients. In one hospital, when the government tried to forbid such activity, the deaconesses said they would quit rather than stop singing and praying. It didn't take long for the authorities to give in because they desperately needed the skills and dedication of the nurses. I decided I would visit the deaconesses while at the Bible conference.

But as I drove along with my partner, Erik, I heard on the radio about a startling development: The communist government had begun to erect a wall of concrete and barbed wire between East and West Berlin. Sure enough, in West Berlin we had to pass through what would later be called Checkpoint Charlie, with its foreboding display of soldiers, machine guns, and guard towers.

At the time Erik and I had a rather cavalier attitude toward the new wall. As we safely got through, he even said, "Andrew, that was fun—let's go back and do it again."

This guy is crazy, I thought.

As it turned out, I was crazier still because I did turn around to do it again. Nothing happened. (We weren't carrying any Bibles because at that time the church there had no need for them.)

Once inside East Germany, however, I saw a much darker picture of the Wall's effect. The people were absolutely stunned. Suddenly they were completely cut off from friends, business partners, relatives, and even family members who had happened to live on the free side. Until that point many who did not want to remain in East Germany under the communist regime had been able to get out of the country safely, but now they had little or no hope. I heard many reports of people committing suicide.

The Bible conference went well, with hundreds of believers gathering to pray each morning on the huge conference grounds. Erik and I had a wonderful time staying in the deaconesses' "monastery." But after hearing of so much desperation among the people, even some of the Christians, I determined to visit the country again soon.

Several months later I returned to the Wall with another Dutch colleague, Jan. That time all the eyes of the West were on us, as the news media had focused its cameras on Checkpoint Charlie. It seemed that every house and every building with a view of the gate had cameras perched in open windows and on the roofs, all waiting to capture a dramatic escape on film. Some East Germans were tying themselves under cars and trucks and attempting all sorts of daring feats in order to sneak out of the country, risking imprisonment or execution. There were a few successes and many failures, all heavily publicized.

Again we crossed with no difficulty and traveled to meetings around the country. While there, I heard about a church in one town where the pastor, a godly man, had committed suicide. His death had left the other members devastated, many of them to the point of despair. The young minister who replaced him was too inexperienced to handle the situation, and he begged me to visit.

"One of the elderly sisters in our church has threatened to commit suicide as well," he said over the phone. "Yesterday she told me the devil is stronger than Jesus. Can you please come as soon as possible?" I heard the urgency in his voice.

"Okay, I will come," I told him. "I'm speaking at a meeting in Karl Marx City that night, but we can stop over for a couple of hours on the way."

I had planned to make one more brief stop in a nearby town before visiting the pastor. A family I had stayed with many times had offered to do our laundry for us. Normally I did my own, but my schedule had filled up and I knew it would help if we could simply drop off our sack of dirty clothes and pick it up the next day. When we arrived at the house, the kind woman invited us in for a cup of coffee.

"I'm sorry," I told her, "but we have no time today. Perhaps when we return."

"But I also have needs," she pleaded. "I want to talk about some things. I need your prayer."

So we were persuaded to stay there a little while. Before long I saw it was too late to visit the young pastor on the way to our meeting. So I phoned him and said, "Sorry, but we will come tomorrow morning, first thing."

We had a great meeting that night in Karl Marx City. The topic was spiritual warfare. The next morning we met the young pastor and drove with him over to the troubled sister's house. She lived on the second or third floor of a big apartment building. Jan and I waited downstairs while he went up to let the woman know she had visitors. Within a few seconds he reappeared, ashen faced.

"It's too late—she is dead!" he blurted.

We ran up after him to the apartment. There she was, slumped over on the kitchen floor between the oven and the furnace. The oven door was open, and the whole place smelled of gas. I knew she was dead.

Jan frantically rushed to her side, took her hand, and began to pray that God would perform a miracle and raise her from the dead. I stood there in shock for a moment, trying to take in what had happened. Then I put my hand on his shoulder.

"Jan, stop this," I said, shaking my head. "God will not answer this prayer. We've got to pray for ourselves. We should have been here last night. We could have saved this life. We need forgiveness." So he stopped praying.

It was a very sad experience, but it served as a warning to me: *Be on time. When God calls, or when his people are in need, be there.* It also made me more determined to find others who would join me in upholding our struggling brothers and sisters.

Because I personally witnessed the pain and suffering it caused for so many, I grew to hate the Berlin Wall, as I hate all man-made walls that come between people. When it came down nearly thirty years later, and people were handing out pieces of it as mementos, I had absolutely no desire for one. I had seen the other side of the wall, and I didn't want any part of it.

Yet I also knew that God had mysteriously used that wall to strengthen his church. There can be something good about an Iron Curtain, especially when it drives you into the arms of a loving God. It restricts your freedom, but it also protects you from the some of the harmful things freedom can bring, such as materialism and decadence. It helps you to see what is most important in life—your faith in Christ.

When that wall finally fell, liberty was restored in East Germany. But do you know what else happened? Bible sales plummeted almost immediately, and the church's influence in the society waned considerably. What could have been a time of mobilization for the East German church instead became a time of sitting back and congratulating itself.

—◄o►—

Around the time *God's Smuggler* was published, I went on another very significant trip. I never wrote or spoke about it because at that time everyone's eyes were on Russia, but it awakened my interest in a part of the world that has now become my primary passion: the Muslim world.

I was conducting a seminar at a missions school near Lausanne, Switzerland. There I met a tall Englishman who lived in a cottage on Lake Geneva, and he was doing research for a book about the location of the real Mount Sinai. One day, out of the blue, he asked me if I'd be interested in joining him on an expedition to Saudi Arabia to do more research.

I didn't even know the chap, whose name was—of all things— Lawrence, and I had never been to Saudi Arabia, but I did have a vague interest in the world of Islam, so of course, I said yes. One other man, Doug Sparks of Youth with a Mission, would also accompany us. I should have known that Saudi Arabia was not the place to start—even today—because it is the hardest country for a Christian to make any inroads.

Nevertheless, a few months later, the three of us met at Beirut Baptist Seminary in Lebanon, where we stayed for a few days. My English friend bought a used gray Land Rover there, equipped it for the journey, piled in the boxes of Arabic Bibles I had brought, and we took off. First we drove east to Damascus,

Syria, then headed south on the main road toward Amman, Jordan. My back bothered me a lot during that time, so for most of the trip I would lie on top of the luggage in the backseat and try to sleep.

Was I in for a surprise. Halfway between the Syrian border and the city of Amman, I was suddenly jolted awake by screeching brakes, then knocked to the floor as our car smashed into something. We had just rear-ended someone's big Mercedes. I was thankful that no one was hurt, but the owner of the car was understandably angry. He called the police and, knowing that we were foreigners, demanded that we pay immediately for the damages. I hadn't seen what happened, but apparently the accident had been our fault.

As I watched the men heatedly trying to communicate with each other, I decided I didn't want to wait around for the police. Who knew what they would do or how long we'd be detained? I knew Lawrence and Doug would have to stay behind, but why me? I had been sleeping—I'd be a lousy witness anyway. So I told them I was going to find a ride into Amman, and I gave them the name of a Hospital Christian Fellowship contact I had there. They could pick me up when they worked everything out with the car.

So I left everyone behind and started hitchhiking. We were in the middle of nowhere, but with Amman only an hour away, I didn't have to walk far before someone picked me up.

That same evening I preached twice in a church in Amman and had a great time of fellowship with the believers. I enjoyed catching up with a number of friends I had met on a previous visit.

My traveling companions didn't turn up for another two days, however. They had been taken to the local police station and locked up in a jail cell! They were forbidden to leave until they had paid for all the repairs to the Mercedes. So they had to sit there while the owner got an estimate and Lawrence could arrange to have money wired to him. We had a good laugh together when they recounted their story.

Finally we left Amman in our dented-up Land Rover. As we ventured south toward the Saudi border, my anticipation grew. It was the first time since my army days in Indonesia that I'd traveled beyond civilization as I knew it. The arid, barren land around me could not have been more different from that tropical paradise.

Al 'Aqabah, a small town at the very tip of the Gulf of Aqaba, was our last stop before the border. Sometime after dark we reached the tiny border station. We were allowed into the country, but were then told that our car would be searched. So we watched as they removed and inspected every single item from the vehicle. Of course, they found all the Bibles and the Arabic booklets, which I had made no attempt to hide.

They said nothing about the Christian literature, even though it was considered contraband. They put everything back and told us to come into the office. After a few minutes, I went back to the car to rest in the backseat while Lawrence and Doug talked with the officials.

As I lay there in the darkness, I heard noises outside the car. Two other officials quietly opened the hatchback and began rummaging through our luggage. Either they didn't see me in the backseat, or else they thought I was sound asleep. In any case I was too scared to move or speak. I figured they were just inspecting the car again, but afterward I realized they had stolen a few of our small items and supplies.

Soon I joined the others inside. The official in charge had something to say to us.

"I'm afraid you cannot enter our country because you are driving a military vehicle," he said.

Apparently the Saudi government used Land Rovers in its military at that time. Or else he was just giving us a line—I don't know. Maybe instead of confiscating our Bibles, he preferred to make our visit as difficult as possible.

"Well," I said, "can we turn around and leave then?"

"No, you cannot do that, either," he replied. "You have no exit visa."

Talk about a closed country. You must not only have a visa to get in, but you must obtain another one to get out! We were definitely in a predicament. The officials told us to get back in our car, and then they escorted us a few miles down the road to a huge compound with tall, electric barbed-wire fences. It looked like a prison camp, except that we weren't locked up or interrogated. We were just left there. We could leave if we wanted, but the car would have to stay.

That night we slept fitfully in our car, thinking and praying and trying to figure out what to do. In the morning I set out early on foot toward the city of Tabuk, which I guessed was only a few miles away. A man passing by in a truck offered me a ride. My first stop in town was at the bank to exchange some money for the local currency. Unfortunately the only cash I had with me was a one-thousand-guilder bill, which they had never seen before, so they only gave me seven hundred guilders' worth of Saudi riyals—a little over two hundred dollars.

There was nothing I could do, so I took the money and looked around until I found a taxi that would take us to Jidda, the country's second largest city. The driver first took me back to the compound where my partners were waiting, and we worked out a plan of sorts. Doug would come along with me to Jidda, and Lawrence would stay behind with his car, which he feared would be stolen if he left.

Doug and I went through our luggage and packed all the small Scriptures and gospels of John into big bags to carry with us. If we would never see our vehicle again, I thought, at least we would have most of the Scriptures. Then we said good-bye to

Lawrence, hopped back in the taxi, and headed south. It would be a full day's drive to Jidda.

Six hours later we approached Medina, one of two cities where the prophet Muhammad lived in the seventh century. Mecca, his birthplace, is the other. These cities are so holy to the Muslims that non-Muslims cannot enter them. And just to be sure, signs are posted at the edge of the city that read, INFIDELS FORBIDDEN. A chill ran down my spine as we had to leave the main road and take a bypass route.

Late that evening we made it to Jidda and headed for the international hotel. Only a couple of hotels were operating at that time, and since the oil boom was still years away, prices were reasonable. We spent the next day visiting one of my friends with Hospital Christian Fellowship, now known as Healthcare Christian Fellowship. This Christian man, who ran his own pharmacy, knew of no other believers in the city. Undoubtedly there must have been a few, but there was no way to find them. Churches or Christian gatherings or associations of any kind were forbidden. My visit with him may very well have been the only fellowship he had with other Christians all year.

Doug and I went to the local bazaar afterward and handed out Scriptures to the curious shoppers. To our amazement, no one stopped us. It was probably the first and last time anyone got away with public Bible distribution in Saudi Arabia.

After another day of plodding from office to office, we were able to obtain exit visas and arrange for a flight to Beirut. We had planned to stay in the country for a while and really explore, but because we ran into such trouble, we decided to return home after three days. At least we had gotten a taste of Arab and Muslim culture. We had also witnessed the extreme difficulty of being a Christian in such a place.

We arrived at the Jidda airport early the following morning, before the bookstalls and newsstands had opened. Taking advantage of the empty racks, Doug and I covered them with all of our remaining Scriptures, arranging them in an attractive display. Then we boarded our plane.

Just before takeoff, an announcement came over the PA system: All passengers were to exit the plane immediately.

Oh, no—they've found our Scriptures and they're coming after us, was my first reaction. It turned out to be some problem with the plane, and soon we reboarded and took off for Beirut.

What became of our English friend with the Land Rover? Lawrence had to travel a full day's journey to Riyadh, the capital city, in order to complete all sorts of paperwork. He finally obtained an exit visa but was not allowed to take his car. It took him nearly eight months after returning home to get it back. Other than the few small items that had been pilfered when we first entered, nothing else in the car was missing.

The experiences of that early visit to the Muslim world stayed with me. I started to pray about how God would open the door for me and others to take in more Bibles and build up the scattered believers. When the oil rush began in 1973, and prices jumped from six dollars to thirty dollars a barrel, more and more foreign investors were allowed into the country, and the Saudis had a lot more money to spend. A massive change was taking place in the Arab world, the effects of which we are still feeling today and will continue to feel for many years. It would be a while before I'd devote a large part of my life to taking the gospel to Muslims, but I had the distinct feeling that the time would come.

◄○►

From the earliest days of my ministry, whether in Eastern Europe or the Middle East, I have seen again and again the Bible's power to change people from within. It is a far more effective weapon against communism and other anti-Christian philosophies than any political or military action. Who knows what changes were wrought in people's lives by the Scriptures we left in Saudi Arabia? The power of the Bible is simple, but profound. Besides, when we fight repressive regimes politically and militarily, we set ourselves up as an enemy. We give them martyrs to rally around, we fuel their anger, and we intensify their resolve to advance their cause. The result is that we weaken our own.

The only way to change an evil system in a lasting way is from the inside—by building up the church through prayer, encouragement, and especially the Scriptures. It does not require a special calling. To the contrary, it is what being a Christian is all about.

Step One

Listen to God's prophetic Word for today.

If we want to change the world for God, we must start by listening to his word as given in the Scriptures.

Many times in the Old Testament I read, "And the word of the LORD came unto" a certain prophet. The job of the prophets was to listen to what God was saying and then to declare it, in both word and deed, wherever God told them to go. Most of the prophets in the Bible were not specially trained or highly educated men who received a call during their last year of seminary. By and large they were ordinary people—like you and me—who were following God in their everyday lives. And yet when they spoke God's message, they were able to raise up and bring down entire kingdoms. Their ministry came to have great impact.

To be *prophetic* today does not require us to have an audience with world leaders. It simply means carrying out Jesus' Great Commission to "go and make disciples of all nations" (Matthew

28:19). We do this in response to the prompting of the Holy Spirit through the Scriptures. Put another way, we are prophetic when we meet three conditions:

1. *We know God and his character as taught in the Bible.*
2. *We have a message that will affect people's lives.*
3. *We have somewhere to say it.*

Since the Old Testament prophets didn't have the Bible, they had to hear their message directly from God. Today we can look to his written Word to know him and his will for us. As we saturate ourselves in the Scriptures and in prayer, our relationship with Christ deepens. And through the Bible he will begin to impress upon us just how and where he wants us to share his message.

God spoke to me on my first trip to the communist world through a couple of verses in Revelation 3. "Strengthen what remains," he said to the struggling church in Sardis in verse 2. And in verse 8, he told the church in Philadelphia, "I have placed before you an open door that no one can shut." Neither of these passages says, "Andrew, I am appointing you to be a Bible smuggler to Russia." But because I was already studying the Bible, praying, and sharing my faith with those around me, and I had the willingness to go wherever God wanted me, those verses awakened me to the vast need of Christians behind the Iron Curtain. That's how the ministry of Open Doors came into being.

As we spend time in Scripture and in prayer, it's important not to get sidetracked in trying to determine whether we've received an official call from God or whether we have a clear indication that we are doing God's will. It's too easy to get so caught up in the paralysis of analysis that we fail to act.

Most of us often have the idea that God must have a special calling on our lives, a particular end for us to accomplish, and we must find out what it is for us. If we have no such calling from God, then we have not been selected by him for special service, and we can only live out our lives as drones in the kingdom, one monotonous and unimportant day at a time. But we need to understand that that is our idea, not God's.

We must never make our dreams for success or accomplishment as God's purpose for us; his purpose may well be just the opposite. God's end, his purpose for us, is the process. It is today that he wants us to focus on. Oswald Chambers put it so well when he said, "God's training is for now, not presently. His purpose is for this minute, not for something in the future. We have nothing to do with the afterwards of obedience; we get it wrong when we think of the afterwards. What men call training and preparation, God calls the end. . . . If we realize that obedience is the end, then each moment is precious."

A man once approached the great preacher Charles Spurgeon with a question. "There's a Bible verse I read that's bothering me because I can't understand it," he said.

"You should be happy to have such a problem," Spurgeon replied. "It's all those Bible verses I *do* understand that bother me!"

God has given us in Scripture a full revelation of his nature and his character. And he has given us an unmistakably clear mandate to share him and his Word with those who have not heard. What more do we need? If we focus on obeying him on a daily basis—wherever we are—he will lead us where he wants us to go, and to the people he wants us to reach.

Now if we look a little more closely at where the biblical prophets were told to take their message, we gain further insight into what it means to be prophetic. In most cases they were sent into situations where their message would not be well received. Where they had to go against the grain of the popular culture. Where they often had to face severe consequences for proclaiming God's message. Where they were frequently ridiculed as fools.

We can all ask ourselves: Am I willing to carry God's message to this kind of place? Further, am I aware that my own office or school, perhaps even my own home, could be this kind of place?

In London I've seen what they call a sandwich man—a guy who hangs a big poster across his front and back painted with a Bible verse. It's not exactly my preferred method of evangelism, but it sure does grab your attention. One sandwich man I heard about had the verse "I am a fool for Christ" written on the front. As people looked at him, they probably agreed. But when they passed him and turned to see what he'd written on the back, the message was, "Whose fool are you?"

Everyone is a fool for somebody—be it Marx, Mao, Muhammad, or simply Myself. So why not be a fool for Christ?

PRAYER

Lord, cause me to hear your prophetic Word for my life today. And lead me to the places and people who need to receive that Word—even at the risk of being thought a fool.
Amen.

Chapter Two

◄○►

"You Can't Do That!"

*I*f there's anything that can quickly quench the Spirit, it's probably these four words: *"You can't do that!"* We must actively resist this attitude if we are to go where God wants us to go and do what he wants us to do.

People have been saying those words to me all my life, even before I knew there was a suffering church. Back in 1953 while I attended the Worldwide Evangelism Crusade (WEC) missionary training school in Glasgow, Scotland, I needed to find a place to go for the Christmas holidays. I couldn't return home to Holland because I had no money, and we weren't allowed to remain on the campus.

I had spent much of the fall semester in bed with a back problem, and I had found solace in the writings of the late Oswald Chambers—especially his classic, *My Utmost for His Highest.* I had even written to his wife, Biddy, about the blessing I had received. In her reply she had invited me to visit her home in the south of England sometime. So as the Christmas holidays drew near, I phoned her, and she told me I was welcome to stay there. I didn't mention it to anyone; I just went.

When I got back to school in January and sat down at the dinner table with the whole group, Stuart Dinnen, the director, said, "So, where've you been, Andrew?"

I said I had stayed with Oswald Chambers's family.

"What?" he said. "You can't do that!"

"Maybe not," I replied with a smile, "but I just did it."

To me it was nothing special. But to them it was strange. You do not just go and visit the family of a great spiritual man such as Oswald Chambers. Nor do you get up and go to a country that has declared itself closed to the message of Christ.

But why not? I've been doing it all my life.

Now that I think about it, the Bible is full of ordinary people who went to impossible places and did wondrous things simply because they decided to obey God, even when others said, "You can't do that." They weren't any more qualified for their tasks than we are. But they trusted God to open the doors and give them the power they needed in their particular situations.

Joseph go to Egypt as a slave boy and rise to the rank of second in the kingdom? "You can't do that!"

Moses part the waters of the Red Sea? "You can't do that!"

David the shepherd boy defeat Goliath with nothing but a sling and a few pebbles? "You can't do that!"

Jonah travel to the decadent city of Nineveh and with one sermon bring the entire population to repentance? "You can't do that!"

Maybe not, but with God's help, they did it anyway.

And so can we, wherever we are or wherever God leads us. The door may seem closed, but it's only closed the way a super-market door is closed. It stays shut when you remain at a distance, but as you deliberately move toward it, a magic eye above it sees you coming, and the door opens. God is waiting for us to walk forward in obedience so he can open the door for us to serve him.

—◄○►—

Two other events influenced my life greatly, both involving published materials. The first was in 1955, just before I graduated from the WEC school. I had gone into the dormitory basement to get my suitcase when I noticed a magazine lying on top of an old box. It was a slick publication with four-color photos of impassioned young people marching the streets of Prague, Warsaw, and Peking. The youths, the article said, were part of a ninety-six-million-member worldwide organization aiming to usher in a better world and a brighter future. The word *communist* did not appear once, though I did see the word *socialist* a few times. At the end was an invitation to attend a huge rally in Warsaw.

God used that magazine to lead me to a place I had never thought of going, to a suffering church that I didn't even know existed. I went to that rally as a representative of Jesus, and afterward my life was never the same.

The second event was the publication of my book, *God's Smuggler,* in 1967. The response exceeded everything I could have imagined. Within a couple of years, sales had mushroomed into the hundreds of thousands, then later into the millions. (It is still in print today, with more than ten million copies sold.) Royalties from the book, along with many gifts, made it possible for us to purchase office and warehouse space, to print or buy Christian literature and Bibles in many languages, to acquire more vehicles to transport Bibles, and to hire mechanics to customize and maintain them.

There was a downside to the book's publication, however, one that came as no surprise to me: I knew I would not be able to return to the Soviet bloc countries for many years without placing my Christian contacts (or myself) in great danger. At first I felt discouraged, but then I realized God might be trying to tell me something. After all, hadn't my wife, Corry, and I prayed at the end of the book that our team would grow from two to twelve to thousands? I was forced to find others to carry on the work in the Iron Curtain countries. So we brought on several new team members who had a heart for the suffering church. They followed up on the contacts I had established, and then organized teams to carry Bibles or training materials and take encouragement to struggling believers.

But what did God have in mind for me? I believe he was saying, "Andrew, my church is suffering behind the Iron Curtain, but it is also suffering in other countries of the world. Look around! You need to go to these places as well." So I started traveling to other trouble spots of the world where God's people are being persecuted for their faith—China, Africa, Central America, the Middle East. And again, royalties from the book and gifts from supporters made it possible.

As grateful as I am for the success of *God's Smuggler,* one of the reasons for its success bothered me: Almost no one else had been doing what I did. Because I was one of the few people going to these places of great need, somebody wanted to put my story in a book.

But what would have happened if *thousands* of Christians at that time had been risking imprisonment to go to their suffering brothers and sisters behind the Iron Curtain? Probably a book would never have been written—the story would have been common knowledge. But the church worldwide would have grown much stronger as a result. How I wish that so many Christians would stand up and go to where God needs them that nobody will want to write a book about it! Then you or I would never be famous, but at least we would be showing the world what real Christianity is.

━◀○▶━

Our overall approach to a country in which Christians are severely restricted or persecuted is quite simple. First we go there and seek out believers wherever we can find them. We offer encouragement from their brothers and sisters in the free world, and distribute a few Scriptures in their language. We pray with them and worship with them. But mostly we are there to *listen* to them and learn how we can best support them. We ask, "What can we do for you? How can we help? What do you need?"

Inevitably the greatest need is for Bibles. Throughout most of the communist world during the Cold War, Bibles were extremely rare. In the former Soviet Union it was not unusual for a church with hundreds of members to have only one copy of the Bible—if that—for the entire congregation. An occasional copy brought into the country by a relative or friend was considered a prized possession, but they were few and far between.

On the black market a Bible could easily sell for a month's wages, and many desperate Christians would scrimp for months and years to be able to afford one. Others would combine their resources to buy one copy, then break apart the sections and circulate them so each person could have a little portion of Scripture to study and memorize. A minister might arrange to spend his entire two- or three-week vacation with someone who had a Bible so he could copy the text by hand. His hope was that over a period of years he would be able to put together a complete Bible.

We didn't have to hear many of those stories to know of the desperate need for Bibles. So we worked with Bible societies, mission organizations, publishers, and printers to produce Scriptures that could be easily transported and distributed. If the Bible wasn't available in a particular language, or if an existing translation was outdated, we would work with translators to develop a new or revised version. We also experimented with many different sizes, shapes, and portions, usually in an attempt to keep them compact and concealable.

When we were able to return to a country with a load of Scriptures, again and again we would witness expressions of amazement and gratitude on the faces of our Christian friends. Tears would come to their eyes as they picked up a copy and held it close to their hearts.

Years ago I heard a story from Russia that highlighted just how precious a Bible can be in a country with no Bibles. I was speaking at Calvary Church in Denver, pastored by Charles Blair. He had recently traveled to the Soviet Union, and when he introduced me, he told about a pastor and his wife whom he met in a tiny Siberian town. They had wanted to talk to Charles privately, away from the eyes of the police, so they took him out for a ride in their car.

As I listened to him describe the couple, they sounded familiar. During the mid-1960s, when *God's Smuggler* had not yet been published and I was still able to travel in the Soviet Union, I, too, had visited a pastor and his wife in Siberia. But they had owned only a rickety old motorbike; a car was virtually unheard of.

Charles continued his story. The man and the woman were begging him for the one Russian Bible he was carrying with him. Charles couldn't read it, but he was bringing it along to show believers he visited around the country that he loved the Word of God and supported all those who were making Bibles available to the suffering church. When the couple asked him for his only copy, he hesitated, mainly because he had more stops to make in his journey. He wanted to be able to hold up that Bible when he gave greetings to the believers.

But the woman insisted. "Please let me have that Bible," she pleaded. "My daughter is getting married soon, and she will be moving to a very remote area of Siberia where there are no churches and no pastors. She sees this as a wonderful opportunity to be a missionary to the people in her new town. If only she had a copy of the Bible, she could do so much more."

Moved by her need, Charles prayed silently about how to respond. But the woman wasn't finished yet.

"Some years ago," she went on, "another missionary came to us, the first one ever to visit this area. I pleaded with him for a Bible, too. 'I am a medical doctor,' I told him, 'and I am called away to care for patients in many areas far from the city. I visit many dying people, and I want a Bible to read to them about Jesus.' Well, that man gave me his last Bible, and I am still using it today."

She then pulled out an old, extremely worn Bible and showed it to Charles. It had obviously been carried everywhere, read and reread countless times. As he flipped through it, he noticed an inscription on the inside of the cover. Then his eyes widened. The inscription was signed, "Brother Andrew."

At that point Charles knew exactly what God wanted him to do.

As I sat there listening to Charles tell this story, my eyes filled with tears of joy. Who could say how many lives were won to Christ because of that doctor and the Bible I was able to give her? And who knows how many more lives her daughter will influence for Jesus now that she has her own copy of the Scriptures?

--<o>--

I could tell you story after story of God's miraculous work among our Bible delivery teams in Russia and Eastern Europe. Sometimes they went as tourists, sometimes as businesspeople, sometimes as educators or social workers. But in almost every case God performed some kind of miracle that allowed them to take their precious cargo into the country safely. It actually became a guessing game for us at times when we would pray and then wonder aloud, "How is God going to do it this time?"

One team, a pair of young men, was driving one of our specially equipped vans loaded with seven hundred Bibles through Yugoslavia and into Bulgaria, where they had arranged to make a delivery. Their traveling papers indicated they were tourists. While in Yugoslavia they stopped at a lake to take a swim. They also unpacked an inflatable canoe I had bought earlier and took it out on the lake. When they were finished, they didn't bother to let the air out of the boat; they shoved it into the back of the van and forced the back doors shut.

When they reached the Bulgarian border, two officers approached the van. One looked at their papers while the other went around to the back to inspect the luggage. But when the officer opened the rear door of the van, the rubber boat sprang out and popped him right in the head!

He just stood there for a minute, stunned, while the two young men jumped out of the car and ran to his aid. They apologized profusely and politely helped him stuff the boat back into the car and close the door securely—and that was the end of the inspection. Of course, you can never arrange it that way or do it a second time; it just "happens."

On another occasion, one of our Dutch teams was heading into Czechoslovakia. Before reaching the border, they stopped for prayer and—being good Dutchmen—a stiff cup of coffee. One of them opened a carton of condensed milk to pour in the coffee but forgot to put it away afterward. He left it sitting right on top of a box that contained Bibles and a few tools.

At the Czech border, while they were inside the station processing their papers, an officer went out to check the van's contents. He had hardly looked inside when he accidentally knocked over the forgotten carton, spilling milk on the floor of the van. So he ran inside, got a towel, went back to the car, and cleaned up the mess—after which he apologized to the men and quickly sent them on their way.

Yet another team, two young women dressed as if they were going on holiday, approached the border crossing of Czechoslovakia. In their car was a large supply of Bibles. When the officer approached, they exuded a lighthearted, carefree spirit. But then he asked them a direct question, one they could not avoid: "Do you have any Bibles in this vehicle?"

The women had less than an instant to come up with an answer. They didn't want to lie because they did not feel that was God's way. And if they hesitated, they would also be suspect.

So what did they do? They immediately burst into laughter.

"Why, yes," said the driver, giggling. "Our car is *full* of Bibles!"

Apparently the guard thought she was joking; he waved them through.

These miracles may seem small, but I happen to believe that there are no small miracles. Every miracle is big. Every miracle is an act of God based on his truth and designed to carry out his will.

◄○►

Our preferred method of getting Scriptures to churches behind the Iron Curtain was to send in teams to deliver them personally to a known and trusted contact in the church. First and foremost, this approach assured that we were getting Scriptures directly into the hands of Christians who needed them. And we were usually able to fellowship, worship, and pray with our brothers and sisters as well, even if in secret. The courier system worked quite satisfactorily, making it possible for many thousands of Bibles to reach people who were starved for the Word of God.

We did not have qualms with the idea of concealment or smuggling. When human laws forbid us to share our faith or distribute the Scriptures to other believers, we are not bound to obey those laws. We must obey God rather than man. Yet I do not believe it is right to lie in order to carry out God's purposes. It is not the King's way. Instead we have learned to be "as shrewd as snakes and as innocent as doves" (Matthew 10:16). To answer all the queries I received about the ethics of smuggling, I wrote a little booklet that was later incorporated into the book *Is Life So Dear?*

During some of my border crossings, I was asked, "Do you have any religious books in this car?" I immediately replied, "No, none at all." Because I do not consider the Bible to be a book about religion. It is about a way of life, the abundant life Christ gives us when we allow him to live in our hearts.

A major reason the courier system worked was that it wasn't really a system. To avoid detection, we did everything as randomly as we could. Trips and border crossings were scheduled at different times and places. The teams varied, and they always traveled as individuals, friends, or married couples on holiday, or small tour groups. No one ever carried any form of Open Doors identification or information. Most of the contacts we worked with did not even know about the organization, though some of them knew me from my earlier visits. If we found out that some other group was also using one of our contacts, for security reasons we usually moved on and established new ones. We wanted the fewest possible links so our operations could not be traced by police.

Of course, all of this would have come to naught had we not bathed every person and every aspect of our operation in prayer. Total, absolute dependence on God was and is the only way we can accomplish anything for him.

But at the same time we were constantly brainstorming and trying out new ways to take the good news across the closed borders. We cooperated with missions such as Trans World Radio, radio station HCJB, and the Far Eastern Broadcasting Company, which transmitted gospel radio messages across Eastern Europe and throughout the Soviet Union. Many listeners would write to the stations and tell of their suffering and their great needs, and we would sometimes provide follow-up materials to send or deliver to them through our networks.

One approach we took was to invite friends of Open Doors to join official tourist groups traveling to Russia. We would then supply Bibles for them to take in their luggage. I remember one guy, John, who years ago got a bit carried away with this idea but stumbled into a wonderful opportunity. Fluent in seven languages, including Czech and Russian, he was booked on a tour group with communists and others to Russia. But he was so eager to take as many Bibles as possible with him that he showed up at Schiphol Airport in Amsterdam looking quite plump and walking stiffly. He had stuffed all his clothing with Russian Bibles, literally from top to bottom! He'd even worn a customized pair of long underwear with forty Bible pockets sewn on. He must have looked absolutely ridiculous.

At the airport, John learned that many people in the tour group had canceled. The year was 1968, and Russian troops had just moved into Czechoslovakia a couple of weeks earlier. Political tensions were high, and people didn't want to take the risk. In fact, when he checked in at the desk, John found that so many people had called off the trip that the communists who were supposed to lead the tour had also backed out. So the travel agent looked around and, discovering that John was fluent in Russian, made him the tour leader. Because a tour leader had much more freedom than the other members of the group, that gave him tremendous opportunities.

But there was still the matter of all those Bibles he was carrying. On the plane to Leningrad, he got so sweaty and overheated from his heavy Bible "insulation" that the customs officials singled him out for a health check when they landed. Somehow, thank God, he managed to talk his way out of the inspection. It was a scary experience for him, a narrow escape. But once he got into the country, he was able to deliver his Bibles, arrange interesting meetings, and introduce other people to the churches—things he never would have been able to do had he not been the tour leader.

You wouldn't believe some of the other ideas we came up with. We considered sending up helium balloons to float across the borders carrying packages of literature, but found them too hard to control. We thought about using ultralight aircraft to fly in at low altitude, underneath the communist radar, and make Bible drops. I was so excited about that idea that I even took a test flight on an ultralight to see how feasible it was. We decided it was too risky and inefficient. But what about sending in a smaller, remote-controlled ultralight? Possibly, but we'd lose the personal contact, and we'd also want to be able to destroy the craft if something went wrong. That would mean explosives, and we didn't want to get involved with those.

At one point we considered an underwater Bible delivery using a submarine. We had learned from a few Russian believers about a virtually unguarded stretch of beach in one of the Baltic States. A small submarine, similar to the ones used by scientists to study the ocean floor, could be sent in with a load of Scriptures. It could surface near the beach, and local Christians with a few small boats could row out and transfer the cargo. For a variety of reasons we ended up scrapping the idea, but it came up again years later, as we shall soon see, in the initial planning stages of Project Pearl, where we delivered a million Bibles to China by sea.

Our attitude was, if you really want to do it, you do it. You find ways. We always found ways and kept on searching for new ones. I believe the Lord has honored that attitude.

—<o>—

Throughout the Cold War years, our teams were able to take Bibles into nearly every Soviet bloc country. Some, such as Yugoslavia, were fairly easy, while others, such as Romania, proved more difficult. There was only one country that was almost impossible to penetrate: the ultrarepressive Albania. Its staunch Stalinist leader, Enver Hoxha, was so oppressive that he had severed relations with the Soviet Union and later China because he felt their governments were too lax. During the 1960s, he set out to eliminate all religion of any kind from the country, and in 1967, he boldly declared Albania the world's first truly atheistic state.

I had challenged my workers at home not to give up on that country. "If you want to make an impact on the world for Christ," I told them, "you've got to do it somewhere that will grab the attention of the whole world. I suggest that you choose Albania." Several of our people had visited the country, but it, like China, was one of the only places that you could not "accidentally" leave your Bible behind in your hotel room. They would run after you and give it back.

Once in the early seventies I spoke for Youth with a Mission's Discipleship Training School in Switzerland, and I challenged them about Albania. Several young women were moved to go there and discreetly share the gospel. One of them, Reona Peterson, got very sick while there and had to be cared for by a nurse in her hotel room. She thought she recognized something of Jesus in that nurse's face, and felt she could trust her, so she gave her a copy of John's gospel in Albanian.

She was mistaken. The nurse immediately reported her, and she was arrested, put on trial, and sentenced to death—all for handing out a single copy of the gospel of John. On the day she expected to be executed, she was taken out and dumped over the border into Yugoslavia.

So we decided to take it slow, occasionally sending people in as travelers. Then we set up a business and went there to buy folding chairs, hoping that we'd make a few friends and build bridges. It didn't work.

Later on, the door opened for a very restricted form of tourism. So we at Open Doors decided to organize prayer teams that would simply drive around the country and pray. No witnessing, no Bibles, no literature, just praying over the cities and towns. It's a thoroughly biblical concept. In the Old Testament God told Joshua, "I will give you every place where you set your foot" (Joshua 1:3). So the teams walked and prayed.

There is no question in my mind that God used every one of those people, every one of those prayers, to bring down the oppressive system in Albania. Even when we can't talk about our faith or openly give out Scriptures, we can still be there. It's an important thing to remember, perhaps even the most important thing.

Step Two

◄o►

Plan to do today what Scripture says.

A few years ago when I had a sore throat, I drank some of those herbal teas from California with little sayings printed on the tags. One of them said, "If you ain't the lead dog, you always have the same scenery."

Okay, maybe it's a little naughty, but I was struck by the truth in that statement when applied to our spiritual calling. Jesus told his disciples—and us—to go into all the world as his witnesses (Acts 1:8). Keep in mind that in Jesus' time the world was quite hostile to the good news, so much so that the people put Jesus to death. Jerusalem, Judea, Samaria—these places were as closed as any closed country is today. Yet his disciples were told to go anyway.

They had to be the pioneers, in other words, the "lead dogs," if you will. The pioneer has to know where he is going, and that takes planning. If we don't push into new mission fields and go where we are *needed* rather than where it is safe, we'll end up seeing the same old scenery, clinging to our same old theories, and doing things the same old ways they've always been done. And we won't get any closer to fulfilling the Great Commission to tell the world about him.

Jesus said to the disciples, "Open your eyes and look at the fields! They are ripe for harvest" (John 4:35). If a farmer doesn't plan carefully, often years ahead of time, he'll never harvest a crop. Farming is a science, where every step from plowing to harvesting must be considered and adequately planned for. Sharing Christ is the same way.

Look at the fields! Look at China. Look at the Muslim world. Look at Cuba. Look at some of the countries in Africa, Latin America, and South America. Look at the people in your office, your neighborhood, your school. They are ripe for the harvest, but if we're going to make an impact for Christ there, we will have to plan. We must plan to act on the prophetic Word we received in step one.

Jesus also said to his disciples, "I sent you to reap" (John 4:38). All too often we in the church have been willing to sow, but when it comes to reaping, we use pious phrases to avoid it: "That's not my calling." "Reaping is God's work." In the meantime, the world is so needy, so open, so ready!

According to Hebrews 10:7, the incarnation of Jesus Christ resulted from a planning meeting in heaven. Jesus came into the world with a plan: To destroy the works of the devil. To reconcile the world with God. And how would he accomplish this? By dying and rising from the dead. I am fascinated by Jesus' prayer to his Father in John 12:27: "Now my heart is troubled, and what shall I say? 'Father, save me from this hour'? No, it was for this very reason I came to this hour." Jesus' determination to do the will of God came out of his resolute planning.

What a terrible thing that so many Christians live without a plan for their lives. I'm not talking about a rigid schedule of life's events, but an active response to the prophetic Word from God that we heard in step one. Whether we believe God is sending us to the jungles of Africa or the jungles of corporate America, we need to respond by intentionally planning where we want to go and how to reach those Christ wants us to reach, knowing that whoever is reachable is winnable.

Until I made that first trip to the Socialist Youth rally in 1955, I didn't have a specific plan for my life. I had never even heard of Bible smuggling. At that point all I knew was that I wanted to be a missionary. What kind of missionary? Where? That was up to God. So I pursued that general goal the best I could by attending the WEC school in Scotland, and I trusted God to reveal the next step to me along the way.

Sure enough, he planted that socialist magazine in the basement of my dorm where I could stumble across it, and the rest is history. Once I'd taken that trip, there was no turning back. From that point on I planned my life in the direction of serving the suffering church.

What then is the purpose of your life? And what part does that purpose play in fulfilling the Great Commission? That's where the planning comes in.

At the spiritual level, planning means taking the initiative. It's not about sitting around until you are absolutely certain God is calling you to a particular task, direction, country, or ministry. Nor is it waiting for the doors to open so you can go there easily. Planning is an act of faith. Jesus never told his disciples to wait for an invitation. He told them to go. Where and when will often arise out of your time in the Scriptures. After all, as D. L. Moody said, it's not how many times you have gone through the Word, but how many times it has gone through you.

At the practical level, planning means research. Before I go into a country, I need to know: What are the political, economic, and spiritual conditions in the place I want to go? How many Christians are there? Are they allowed to practice and share their faith openly? What kind of persecution are they experiencing? How and where can I meet other believers? What are the specific needs of the church—Bibles, literature, training, hard-to-obtain equipment, money? What are the best ways for me to help them meet those needs? Would I be reduplicating or complementing the work of others?

An excellent place to begin this research is Patrick Johnstone's book *Operation World,* a regularly updated overview of every country in the world from the standpoint of Christian missions. Besides providing valuable statistical information for each country, the book identifies spiritual and material needs and offers suggestions for prayer. It is truly a world awareness workbook.

Other ways to conduct research might be talking with present or former missionaries from the country (if they exist), or present or former citizens who are Christians. We can also learn a great deal by talking with foreign students who are attending school in our country. Even a brief holiday visit to the place of interest would be a valuable information-gathering experience. And we need to keep abreast of current events via the news media.

This does not mean, however, that the only mission fields are far away. We should be conscious every morning, from the moment our feet hit the floor, that we can and will bring Christ's presence into the relationships of our daily lives.

On the inside cover of my Bible, I have pasted an interesting quote: "Either a man must be challenged or he must be entertained." God's Word is not meant to entertain us. It is not even intended to make us happy. Rather, it is intended to make other people happy *through* us—when we accept the challenge God has given us to fulfill the Great Commission in whatever circumstances we find ourselves in.

The bottom line? If we are passive rather than active, always waiting for doors to open rather than stepping out in faith, then we are not planning to reach the world for Christ.

PRAYER

*Lord, help me to accept your prophetic Word today and plan my
life based on it.
Allow me to take the initiative in advancing your kingdom, and
keep that initiative even in enemy territory.
Amen.*

Chapter Three

◄O►

One Life to Give

T he atheistic philosophy of communism continued to spread during the 1960s and 1970s. I saw it stretching across the world in a great arc from China through the Soviet Union, Eastern Europe, and Africa, and then across the Atlantic to Cuba, where it had established its first Western base of operations.

When I first traveled to Cuba in the mid-1960s, I was struck by the relatively upbeat atmosphere of the country. In contrast to the drab colors of Russia and Eastern Europe, the people of Havana dressed in vivid reds, yellows, and greens. I remember watching a man play the guitar on one of the boardwalks overlooking the shoreline. Most churches and seminaries—even the Bible Society—remained open. While riding a bus with a group of local Christians, I was surprised to hear the young people singing gospel choruses. Overall I sensed that the Cubans were happy people, that their spirits had not yet been beaten down.

I reminded myself that the revolution in Cuba was still young. Similar conditions had existed in Eastern European countries for several years after the communists came into power. But then, the government began taking away people's religious freedoms, one by one. Police would infiltrate churches and religious organizations. Further printing or distribution of Bibles would be forbidden. Churches would face restrictions prohibiting evangelism outside the building, barring the teaching of children, requiring all members to register with the police, and so on.

As the government pressure increased, many church buildings would be closed, key pastors would be imprisoned or discredited, known Christians would lose their jobs or face demotion, and their children would lose their chance to attend a university. Any churches that remained open usually had agreed to cooperate with the government. Schools would indoctrinate the children in Marxist teachings and urge them to abandon their religious faith.

Pastors and priests seemed to experience the most persecution. Since they were considered nonproductive members of society, they did not qualify for food stamps and were often forced to spend long hours in the fields cutting sugarcane. But they were still allowed to remain pastors, and their churches stayed open.

Among Christians in general, repression certainly took place, but in somewhat milder forms, usually harassment. Even those were having their effect, however. The large church building in Havana where I held a series of meetings had once been a thriving congregation, but that was before the antireligious campaign. Crowds would gather outside the church, shouting and blasting anti-God propaganda over loudspeakers. Heavy construction equipment would suddenly appear on Sunday mornings and launch into a noisy clatter of street "repairs." Police infiltrated the membership. By the time I visited in 1965, this church had only two members left on its register.

No sooner had I arrived at my hotel than the local authorities called me in for questioning. What was I doing there? they wanted to know. And why were there Russian and Czech and East German visas stamped on my passport?

I decided to be straightforward. "I've come to preach the gospel," I said.

For some reason—I can't imagine why—my answer failed to calm their suspicions. They pelted me with questions for the next few hours, and then ordered me to report back for the next three days for more interrogation. Eventually they must have decided I wasn't a spy because they stopped calling me into the station. But they did keep an eye on me, and they sent plainclothes police to attend the meetings at the large church.

Thirty-five people showed up the first two nights—a lot, considering the harassment they had to endure. The next two nights there were sixty. By the end of the week more than a hundred came to hear my gospel messages. In one meeting I preached on John 10 and stressed the need for shepherds to remain with their flock rather than run away. I was referring to the temptation many persecuted Christians feel to leave their country at the first opportunity. Unfortunately, when they leave, they often get swept up in the materialism and decadance of the free world and lose their faith. And the struggling church they leave behind grows even weaker. In Cuba, Fidel Castro had permitted a tiny number of citizens to emigrate each year, and the waiting list numbered into the hundreds of thousands.

At the end of my sermon, one man stood and told the congregation that he was a Methodist minister who had applied to leave for America, but he had changed his mind and was going to stay. There was work for him to do in Cuba—God's work. Another couple I met later had already purchased their plane tickets to leave, and God had spoken to them, too. "Our mission field is right here," they said.

Indeed it was. And in the following years, it would become an even greater one. So I focused my energy on warning them of what was ahead and helping them to plan for a response. How would they hold fast to their faith amid government pressure to compromise? How would they organize meetings for worship and fellowship if their buildings were taken away? Where would they find the Bibles, the literature, and the training they needed?

I went back to Cuba several years in a row during that period, staying a full month each time. Each year the Christians' plight worsened. The second year I visited, the Bible Society was closed down and the director thrown in prison, so no more Scriptures would be printed. That was an area I could help with, so I organized a series of courier trips to supply Bibles. Shortly after that, the president of the Baptist seminary was also imprisoned, though the seminary remained open. (Why not? An open seminary with no president and no students poses no threat.)

Another year the government announced a nationwide literacy campaign. It's always good for people to learn to read and write, even if the communists use it for propaganda purposes. Why? Because the more people are literate, the more they can read and understand the Bible as well. Unfortunately the campaign had a dual purpose—not only to raise the literacy rate but to cripple the churches. The plan: Close all schools and churches for a number of weeks, and send the oldest kids—teenagers— out into the countryside to teach everyone how to read and write.

I never heard whether the literacy rate greatly improved in Cuba, but what I did hear broke my heart. At the conclusion of the campaign, almost none of those kids went back to church. Many of the girls had gotten pregnant and because of their shame either married quickly or moved to another part of the country. In any case, few of them returned to their congregations. When I learned of that lost generation of young people, I grew all the more determined to help strengthen the church in Cuba.

Of course, the government had become increasingly opposed to my presence in the country as well. On one visit I asked to meet with Castro himself, but he was too busy "out in the sugar-cane fields." So instead I sat down with his minister of culture who, as it turned out, orchestrated much of the persecution against Christians. A true zealot for the revolution, he was not particularly happy to see me.

"I know all about your trips to this country and what you've been doing here," he said bluntly. He held up a thick file of police reports on all the places I'd gone and the people I'd seen on previous visits. "From now on, you are *not* to preach here anymore."

I'd been issued this order many times in my travels. But I refused to accept it. "If I am not allowed to preach, sir," I replied, "then would you object if I asked questions of the people?"

"Well . . . ," he said, pausing for a moment, "I suppose there would be no harm in your doing that."

Carefully I tried to bring him one step farther. "And suppose the people wanted to ask me a few questions? Can I answer them?"

Still another pause. "I don't believe that would cause any problems."

That was all the permission I needed. Within his guidelines, I could basically say whatever I wanted.

In hopes of building a bridge to him, I continued the conversation. "Sir, do you realize that if the church in Russia had been truly Christian, there would never have been a revolution?"

"I certainly do," he retorted. "And I don't have to tell you how pleased I am that many Christian churches around the world are not very Christian. Because of that, our revolution will continue to spread. Nothing will stop it. We have one aim—to win this world. But you people often seem more concerned with pie in the sky."

He had a point there.

"I can only respect a Christian if he tries to win me to his cause," he added with a smirk. "But thankfully there are not too many like that."

For the rest of my visit, whenever I stood up in church to speak, I would begin by saying, "I have a few questions to ask of you. What do you think it means to be a follower of Christ in today's world? How many of you have accepted Jesus Christ as your Savior?" One by one, people in the congregation would share enthusiastically about the Christian life and their own relationship with Jesus. Then, after a while, I would say to them, "Now, do you have any questions for me to answer?" Hands would shoot up, and someone would ask, "How can I be born again?" Another person would say, "What does the Bible teach us about who Jesus really was?" After listening to a few questions, I would take all the time I needed to open up the Scriptures and answer them.

Of course, the police still attended the church services, and when they later reported back to the minister of culture, he was infuriated. I knew I would not be welcome in Cuba much longer.

◄o►

Part of the excitement of going to the suffering church is that you never know how God will use you for his glory. Opportunities abound to share the good news with many who don't know Christ, and also to encourage and pray with struggling believers. What's more, when I leave to return home, I always feel that those believers ministered to me!

During my time in Cuba I had a wonderful Christian interpreter, a Jamaican-born man by the name of George. His family had moved to Cuba when he was a child, and he grew up there. He still lives in Havana today. Several years ago he visited Canada and told a remarkable story about one of my preaching tours, a story whose conclusion even I did not know.

I was just getting ready to walk out onto the platform of a church in Havana, and as I looked over the sanctuary, I noticed

George kneeling at the altar, praying earnestly. I had no idea what he was praying about, but from the anguished look on his face I could tell it was important. So I quietly went up behind him, put my hands on his shoulders, and prayed for him silently. That was all, as far as I knew. Then we proceeded with the service, and George did a fabulous job of interpreting.

Now here's the part of the story I recently discovered. George had been suffering from a serious digestive disorder, possibly an ulcer. The pain and stomach cramps he felt were so severe at times that he could hardly finish interpreting a message without having to leave. But he had never mentioned his problem to me.

On that particular night, the stomach pains had started earlier than usual, and he was in such agony that he didn't think he'd be able to make it through the service without losing consciousness. So before the meeting he knelt at the altar and pleaded with the Lord to relieve the pain.

That was the moment God moved me to pray with him.

Even though I did not know what I was praying for, God relieved George's pain almost immediately. Several days later, George noticed it had not returned. In fact, he has never had a problem with his stomach since. George looked back on that incident as a turning point in his spiritual life, one that gave him a new confidence in the power of God. He went on to become a pastor and remains active in the Havana Christian community.

Do you know why I love hearing that story? Because I had no idea what was going on. That is the adventure of going where God leads you and trusting him to work through you. George's healing had nothing to do with Brother Andrew. It could have been anyone. It could have been you.

—◦—

Besides providing lots of Scriptures for the Cuban church, we sought ways to help pastors and their families survive in the country's collapsed economy. I already mentioned that pastors were denied the usual stamps to purchase food and clothing. And if they were in prison—as many pastors were by that time—their families would need to be supported. The currency was nearly worthless, so giving them money didn't help. The Dutch ambassador had given us access to the diplomatic shop in town, where I could use dollars to buy them bedsheets, clothing, gasoline, and some food. But still it wasn't enough.

Then the pastors gave us an idea. On the street, gold was a much more valuable and stable form of currency. If we would be able to bring them jewelry and other items made of gold, they could get a much higher price and support themselves for longer periods of time. One three-hundred-dollar gold watch purchased in the U.S., for instance, might provide six months of income in Cuba. So on one of my last visits, my partner and I and several other couriers wore all kinds of gold watches and rings and bracelets and necklaces. We looked like playboys.

I invited a group of pastors to my hotel and treated them to a meal. They kindly accepted but asked me if I could provide plastic bags for them to take some of the food back to their needy families. As we ate, they quietly stuffed some of the chicken and rice and rolls into the bags. Afterward we all made our way to one pastor's house, and I watched as his children gobbled up the food he brought. Then my colleague and I took off the jewelry and laid it out on the table.

"Please, my friends, accept these gifts from the believers of Holland," I said. "Use them to support your families and those of other pastors who are in prison. Remember that we love you and are praying for you." Gratefully they divided it up according to their needs.

When the time came for me to return home, one pastor took me to the José Marti International Airport to say good-bye. He walked with me as far as the customs area, where we would have to part ways. As I turned to leave, I decided to ask him, "Is there anything else you need?"

"Well, yes," he answered quickly. "I need a pair of shoes."

I glanced at his feet, then looked down at my own. We both wore about the same size. Once I got on the plane, I'd just be sitting until I reached Amsterdam. I could easily get another pair of shoes when I got home. So I bent down, removed my shoes, and handed them to him.

"Take them, brother—they are yours."

I'll never forget the look of gratitude on his face. Then I said a simple good-bye and strolled in my socks through customs and onto the plane.

It did not turn out to be a simple flight to Amsterdam. At our stopover in Madrid, there was a long delay and the airline had to put us up in a posh hotel for the night. People gave me some pretty strange looks as I stood in the hotel lobby in my socks. But I could not get out of my mind the words that pastor had said to me as I left Cuba.

"Andrew," he said, "now you have given everything. The only thing you have left to give is your life."

-◄o►-

After my last Cuban visit, I began to challenge others in Europe to go there, too. The church needed all the prayer, support, and literature it could get.

Among those who expressed interest in helping the church in Cuba were Ans and Line, two Dutch women in their late fifties who lived together in the mountains of France. These two wonderful ladies had already taken several courier trips in Europe to deliver Bibles, and their dedication to God truly inspired me. When I suggested that they consider Cuba, they jumped at the idea.

I didn't give them a heavy agenda of activities for their visit. I simply briefed them on the current situation there, gave them some Spanish Bibles and literature, and a couple of names and addresses. I knew that God would show them whatever else they needed to do. By the way, the main contact I gave them was that of a large congregation in Havana known (appropriately) as the Church of the Open Door.

Once they reached Havana, they went to their hotel room and decided to follow the Lord in prayer. As they prayed, they felt the Spirit prompting them to go to Lenin Park, so they took out their map and set out.

Meanwhile, unbeknownst to them, a local pastor by the name of Eusevio Perez was praying, too. He had recently gotten out of prison and was very discouraged, to the point that he wanted to quit the ministry. Pastors were looked down upon and often persecuted by the government, not only because of their faith, but also because they were considered "parasites" of society. Eusevio felt isolated and powerless, and he wondered whether all his effort was worth it.

On that particular day, he felt the Lord telling him in prayer to go to Lenin Park, that someone would be there to encourage him. So he went outside and got into his car—a 1950 Chevy that he called Lazarus because it had to be resurrected so many times —and made his way to Lenin Park.

As he strolled casually through the park, he noticed two European women also walking around. They appeared to be looking for someone. A few moments later, when they made eye contact, he realized that *he* was that someone! The Lord had directed them to each other.

Well, Ans and Line got right down to business. They followed him to his car, climbed into the backseat, and promptly started taking off their clothes! You must understand that in those days, for security reasons you had to carry as much stuff as possible on your person. The women had worn extra layers of clothing to give to people, and they had also stashed Bibles inside the layers. So in the backseat of Lazarus those near-senior citizens tugged and pulled and wriggled until they'd removed all the literature and extra clothes for the believers.

Eusevio was overwhelmed at God's provision. He then drove them back to their hotel, and they gave him additional needed materials. In the course of their conversation he mentioned that while in prison he had heard of a Dutchman by the name of Brother Andrew. The ladies were able to tell him that I was the one who had encouraged them to visit Cuba.

Eusevio's Spirit-directed encounter with those two women re-vived his weakening faith, and he charged back into his ministry with new energy. Years later the government kicked him out of the country because he was leading too many people to the Lord! He now lives in Toronto, where he is a leader among the Spanish Christian community.

◄○►

These two dear women who went to Cuba illustrate the princi-ple I emphasize again and again: If you *believe* in the power of God, and you *go* to the suffering church in faith, God will open the doors. Iron, Bamboo, and Sugarcane Curtains, closed bor-ders, dictators, terrorists—these are not the real obstacles that keep us from serving our suffering sisters and brothers. The big-gest obstacles lie in our own hearts—fear, doubt, selfishness, ma-terialism, complacency, the unwillingness to risk suffering, and a host of other excuses.

I am familiar with some of these excuses. I've had plenty of reasons over the years to quit traveling and resume a "normal" life, whatever that is. In fact, I almost avoided this ministry alto-gether because of one of these excuses: my health.

You see, for many years I suffered with severe back problems. The very month that I entered the WEC missionary training college in 1953, my back "went out." It's called a slipped disk, or a herniated disk in the spine. But in my case, not one but many of my disks became loose, and I found myself in excruciating pain. Often I couldn't comb my hair or put my jacket on. Some-one had to help me put on my socks. Sometimes I would reach the point where I couldn't stand or walk. I'd hang on as long as I could until I'd collapse to the floor or sidewalk in pain. If no one was around, I'd have to lie there until someone found me. Then I'd be carried up to my bed until some of the pain subsided and I could regain my strength. Sometimes I was confined to bed for weeks at a time.

I managed to get through those two years of studies and still perform most of my chores and evangelistic outreaches, though never without pain. But when my back flared up, I was nearly useless. I didn't know what to do. Doctors refused to operate on me; surgery in those days was too risky. People prayed over me, anointed me, and laid hands on me. I had done everything I could think of that a Christian could do. But my body was still a wreck. At times I wondered whether God wanted me to pursue something other than missions—something that wasn't so hard on my back.

One particularly painful day at the Bible school, I happened to read the story of Naaman in 2 Kings 5. Naaman was neither an Israelite nor a believer in the God of Israel, yet the prophet Elisha healed him of his leprosy. I said, "God, if there can be healing for a heathen such as Naaman, certainly there must be healing for this child of yours." I *thought* God was speaking to me through this story.

I emphasize the word *thought* because you do not always know right away if God is speaking to you through a particular passage of Scripture. But I believe it is better to obey when you *think* God is speaking than to disobey when you *know* God is speaking.

Anyway, I felt strongly that God was going to heal me from that awful pain in my back. What's more, I believed God was going to do it just like in that story of Naaman: by dipping myself seven times underwater. In the biblical account, Elisha's messenger told Naaman to dip himself seven times in the Jordan River and he would be healed. Naaman was furious. The Jordan was a filthy river. He could never imagine being healed of anything by jumping into that water. And bathing seven times in it was humiliating. But eventually he swallowed his pride and dipped in the Jordan, and sure enough, God healed him.

So late one winter night, I made up my mind to follow Naaman's example. After everyone was asleep, I quietly rolled out of bed, crawled across the cold floor to the bathroom (I was in too much pain to walk), and locked the door behind me. Inside was a huge old-fashioned cast-iron tub, big enough to hold an entire family. It would serve as my Jordan River.

Making my way to the side of the tub, I turned on the cold water faucet. (Naaman had strongly disagreed with the water, so it had to be cold.) When the tub was full, I managed to hoist myself over the edge and drop into that icy water. The shock to my system nearly stopped my breathing. Then I clumsily climbed out and rested on the floor for a minute. My back hurt more than ever.

I managed to get in and out a second time. Still nothing. Then a third and a fourth. I almost lost consciousness from the pain and the numbing cold, but I knew I had to make it to the seventh dip because there was no change in Naaman until he had done it seven times. Don't ask me how I did it, but somehow I mustered the strength to haul myself in and out seven times. I noticed *some* change in my condition, but unfortunately it was a change for the worse. By the seventh time I thought I was nearly dead. Finally I unplugged the bathtub, dried off the best I could, and dragged myself back to the bedroom. My body was killing me, but my heart was happy because I had done what I *thought* God was asking of me.

The next morning I was anything but healed.

Nor did it happen the following day or the following week or the next two years. When I left that school, and the principal shook my hand, he said, "Andrew, there is no need for you to apply here to be a missionary—you are simply too weak to travel."

And with that brief statement, I was written off.

I have to admit, I was tempted to agree with him. I was a physical wreck. Certainly it would be easy to interpret my condition as an indication from God that I was not cut out for a mobile ministry. Why not let someone else do it, someone with a strong, healthy body who could perhaps be more effective? Those thoughts did occur to me, the way they seem to occur to all of us.

But something in me—and I know it was the Lord—was saying, "Go." Would I listen to that voice? Would I trust him to handle the obstacles, whatever they were, even my health? When I picked up that communist youth magazine in the basement and read about the rally in Warsaw, I knew I had to say yes. I had to go. And so began my extensive journeys throughout the communist world.

My back problem continued for a total of eighteen years. But the Lord eventually did heal me, in 1971. Do you know how?

In a plane crash.

I was in a Beechcraft Debonair with my pilot friend, Don. We were just taking off from the airport in Salida, Colorado, where I had set up a small U.S. office, and we were headed to a meeting in Denver. Don was an experienced bush pilot who'd been flying all of his adult life, so I felt completely confident in his ability.

On that particular morning, a Sunday, we had just left the runway and reached an altitude of four or five hundred feet when—for reasons unknown to us—the engine abruptly quit. Suddenly my stomach leaped into my throat as I felt the plane dropping straight down like a rock.

"What are we *doing*?" I cried out.

"Crashing!" was all Don had time to say.

The plane slammed into the ground on its belly with a deafening crash. An intense pain shot up my spine, but I was otherwise conscious. Don, who had cut his head open, yanked off his seat belt, and shouted, "Andrew, get out and run—the plane could explode at any moment!"

I managed to pull myself from the craft, but as soon as I tried to take any steps I collapsed in agony, unable to move any farther. As I lay there, I noticed that I had fallen right next to a large anthill, and hundreds of black ants were scurrying around me. We were in a field that extended from the end of the airport runway. Just beyond us was a huge ravine. I breathed a prayer of thanks to God for sparing our lives, but the pain in my back was so great that I didn't care if I died or if the plane blew up or if the ants ate me.

Then I heard an ambulance siren and saw flashing red lights. The people in the airport control tower had seen us go down, and they had immediately sent paramedics and a fire crew after us. Before long we arrived at the hospital. Don's head wound wasn't serious, but I had broken two vertebrae in my lower back. I wouldn't be going anywhere anytime soon.

As it turned out, one of the ambulance drivers was a Pentecostal pastor. Upon recognizing me, he phoned two Christian conferences he knew about in which Kathryn Kuhlman and Jamie Buckingham were participants. They stopped in the middle of their respective meetings to pray for me. That meant a lot.

Soon the doctors cleaned me up, put me in bed, and gave me some painkillers so I'd be more comfortable. Then they let me phone my wife, Corry, in Holland.

As soon as I heard her voice, my emotions came loose, and I forgot my usual Dutch stoicism. I started to cry as I told her about the crash and about my broken back. I was in all sorts of pain and I felt terrible. Since I hardly ever talked that way, she guessed that I must be in very bad shape and quickly arranged for a flight to Colorado.

Within a couple of days she was at my side, and though I still felt plenty of pain, my spirits lifted immediately. For the most part, she sat and read the Scriptures to me each day for hours at a time. With my heavy travel and speaking schedule that year, I had not always found enough time to feed and refresh my spirit from the Scriptures. Now I could be alone with Corry and God and the Word of God. What a wonderful time we had together! As I listened to her read, I praised God and shed tears of joy for his goodness. I had a revival in my heart.

At first, I could do nothing but lie in bed with a thick roll under my back. After a few days they wrapped me in a plaster cast, which immobilized my back and relieved much of the pain. Of course, there were the cold plaster and the constant itching, but they were nothing in comparison.

When the hospital chaplain heard I was there, he prayed with me and then brought other patients into my room so I could pray with them. The day I was allowed to get out of bed and into a wheelchair, he "deputized" me as an honorary assistant chaplain and wheeled me in to some of his patients.

I stayed in the hospital for a total of thirteen days. On the last day they took another X-ray, and my doctor, a renowned orthopedic surgeon, examined it closely. To his surprise, the broken vertebrae were healing so well that he could hardly find a trace of the fractures. That was the first thing that told me God was healing me.

"Well," I said, "many people prayed."

So they released me from the hospital, and Corry and I stayed for a few weeks in Don's mobile home nearby. Corry, being a nurse, helped me learn to walk with the huge cast, which went from my armpits to my hips. Then I'd sit outside on a big tree trunk and look westward across the Rocky Mountains toward the Continental Divide. It was absolutely gorgeous, and I was getting some badly needed rest.

Once I returned to Holland, my doctors there made me wear the cast for another two months. But when they finally removed it and I regained my strength, I started doing things I'd never been able to do before. I learned to play golf. I took up running.

I was able to dig in my garden, play tennis, and ride my bicycle, and I do those things to this very day. I never experienced that slipped disk problem after the plane crash.

God is very original in his solutions, isn't he? His ways are not our ways. How could I have guessed that God would use a plane crash to heal my back? Or how could that Cuban pastor have known that someone would meet him in Lenin Park? When instead of worrying about the obstacles we trust God to take care of them, our Christian life becomes much more effective, not to mention much more fun. Then, as problems arise, we can view them as part of the process in which God is teaching us to walk in faith.

Step Three

━◄o►━

Become persistent in prayer.

When we hear God's prophetic Word and then we plan specific ways to act on that Word, inevitably we are driven to our knees in prayer. Why? Because in the process of planning, we quickly see that reaching the world for Christ is a much greater task than anyone can tackle alone. It can happen only with God's help. So, we need to ask for it.

I cannot emphasize strongly enough the importance of time spent in prayer. Jesus got up early every morning to pray. In Luke 6:12, he prayed all night, and then the next day "a great number of people . . . had come to hear him and to be healed of their diseases. . . . The people all tried to touch him, because power was coming from him" (6:17–19). See how the prayer preceded the power? Similarly, in the Old Testament Nehemiah prayed "day and night" for 120 days before asking the king's permission to rebuild the wall around Jerusalem (Nehemiah 1:1, 6; 2:1). How long did it take to actually rebuild the wall? Only fifty-two days. The *real* work was the prayer.

Unfortunately we don't plan to spend that kind of time in prayer nowadays. We live in practice as if we are stronger than Jesus. And as a result, both our relationship with God and our work on his behalf suffer. "The real reason for prayer," Oswald Chambers wrote in *Christian Disciplines*, "is intimacy with our Father." We pray in order to be in relationship with God. And that intimacy colors the content of our prayers. Having an intimate relationship with God makes it possible for us to pray boldly, as Abraham and Moses and Jesus did.

Of the varied ways to pray, there are two we may neglect: to pray *for* and to pray *against*. We begin by praying *for* those around the world who have not heard the gospel, that God would prepare their hearts to hear his message, whether from us or from Christians already there. Then we pray for the church in that country, especially those who are suffering for their faith. We also pray for God's guidance as we make our own plans to pursue his calling in our own arenas.

But another kind of prayer we need to engage in is what I call praying *against*. We need to pray *against* the forces that oppose God's will. If we want to serve the suffering church and spread the message of Jesus in a so-called closed country, we will come upon many obstacles. We need to ask God to remove them.

Too many Christians have gone soft on this second kind of prayer. It's not enough to ask God to bless us and bless the church and bless the missionaries. We have to learn to pray against evil and against evil people! Evil people actively obstruct us from following the true God or set themselves up as God to be worshiped. This includes many political and religious leaders of our time.

In 2 Thessalonians 3:2, Paul says, "Pray that we may be delivered from wicked and evil men, for not everyone has faith." How are we delivered from evil men? If they do not repent and follow Christ, then the only solution is to pray for their removal—not, I would add, for their destruction.

Ed Silvoso has spoken about the need to pray against evil strongholds. He defines a *stronghold* as "a mindset impregnated with hopelessness that causes us to accept as unchangeable something that we know is contrary to the will of God." This calls for a bolder kind of prayer, one that refuses to naïvely accept all circumstances as God's will. Many people and powers and situations in the world are actively opposing his will, and we must be just as militant in fighting them with prayer. If we want to gain the upper hand on evil, we will have to get on our knees and pray—with blood, sweat, and tears.

There's something else I've discovered about this pattern of praying for and against. When I follow it, I don't need to ask for supernatural signs and dramatic miracles. Looking only (or primarily) for the supernatural can easily lead to thrill seeking or even heresy. But when we confidently ask God to carry out his will and remove the obstacles, his answers bring us into the realm of the supernatural. Anything can happen!

Today there are approximately 2.3 million mosques in the world, each issuing a call to prayer five times a day. That means Muslims have 11.5 million prayer meetings every day. That's a real challenge to Christians. Not in the number of prayers, but the *depth* of prayer, the reality of prayer. Prayer that takes hold of the throne of God on behalf of the church in the Muslim world or the communist world or anyplace in which Christians are suffering. And also prayer for my own life, that I will go where God can use me or do today what will bring salt or light into my world.

PRAYER

*Lord, as I plan my life of service to you, I pray **for** the working out of your will in my situation, and I pray **against** every evil force that opposes your will.*
Amen.

Chapter Four

◄O►

Off the Hinges

As our Bible-smuggling work in Eastern Europe and Russia grew, I lifted my eyes beyond the Soviet Union to that vast country of China, with nearly one-quarter of the world's population. If ever there was a closed country, it was China. And yet Christ died for every one of those hundreds of millions of people. Shouldn't they have the opportunity to hear about Jesus and read the Bible? And what about the church in China? Had believers survived the persecution stemming from Mao's "reforms"?

I describe in *God's Smuggler* my first visit there in 1965, when almost no Westerners were allowed to enter. Getting into the country at all was nothing less than miraculous, not to mention bringing a stack of Bibles with me. Yet during my entire visit, I could not locate any committed Christians or persuade even one person to accept a Bible. I left feeling disheartened. Then in

1966, when Mao cracked down on all forms of religion with his Cultural Revolution, I prayed even harder that God would raise up Chinese believers to "strengthen that which remains" of the church in that country.

Little did I know at that time what the church was *really* like in China. Nor did I know that God would answer my prayer in an unusual way. Corrie ten Boom of *The Hiding Place* fame and I had been traveling together in Southeast Asia, and as we talked with other missionaries and Christian leaders in the area, the name of a man with a strong desire to serve the church in China kept coming up. He would later call himself Brother David—the name I will use in this book—and he was anything but Chinese. He was an American ex-marine. How could such a person get very far in reaching the Chinese, especially in an era when they were taught to hate Americans?

But the more I heard about Brother David, the more I wanted to meet him. He had been running the print shop for the Far Eastern Broadcasting Company (FEBC), based in Manila, which beams daily gospel messages into China. And he had been exploring the various border countries in search of people who would store Bibles for delivery into China. So upon returning home, I wrote him a letter inviting him to meet me.

When we finally got together in Holland in March of 1970, I was struck by David's huge, muscular build. Not only had he been a marine, but he'd also played football in the States. He sat down and told me about his faith and his vision for taking Bibles to the Chinese church. He shared with me various Scripture passages that had awakened his call to China, such as Acts 26 and especially Mark 13:10, where the King James Version says the gospel must be "published" to all nations. Though neither of these Scriptures specifically mentions China, I realized that God had used them to speak to Brother David.

He went on to say that he was praying and trusting God for ten million Bibles for China. He didn't know how or how long, but he clearly believed God could do it. And so did I. Ten million represented only 1 percent of the population; certainly God could be trusted for such a "small" number. Yes, it would take time, but it would be God's timing.

As I listened to Brother David describe his initial steps and his visits to the border countries, I was impressed. He was truly committed to the vision God had given him. But he needed to go farther.

"David, you need to go there yourself," I told him.

About a year later I met with him at JFK Airport in New York. He had not yet visited China because of his FEBC obligations, but it was obvious from our conversation that he felt God's urging more strongly than ever. So we spent the day praying and brainstorming about the next steps. By the end of our time together we emerged with two goals. First, we needed to bring together all the various Christian leaders and organizations interested in China.

Second, we needed to find a creative way to get the Scriptures into the hands of the Chinese people. When I had given out Bibles on my previous visit, they had immediately been identified as such and handed right back to me. Some people undoubtedly had no interest, but I knew others refused because they were afraid to be seen with a book that looked so obviously like a Bible. For the most part, the only reading material they were allowed to carry at that time was Mao's Little Red Book, a compilation of his sayings.

As we prayed and talked together, an idea hit us: Why not print a special edition of the New Testament in exactly the same size, color, and format as Mao's Little Red Book? Then it would cause no suspicion when carried in public, either by Christians or by non-Christians.

David, being a printer, seized upon the idea at once. Yes, he would be able to copy all the details and dimensions of Chairman Mao's little book. The resulting New Testament, in simplified Chinese script, would be nearly indistinguishable from it. So that day I placed an order with FEBC, through Brother David, for twenty-five thousand copies of the Jesus Red Book, as we called it. It was an act of faith, since at that point we had no contacts for Bibles inside China.

—◄o►—

Several months after I placed that order for the Jesus Red Books, Brother David joined the Open Doors Asia staff. Though he was not granted his own visa to visit China until 1976, he worked tirelessly during the early seventies to build a network of contacts, both outside and inside China. In the border countries he and his coworkers located Chinese Christians who had friends or relatives inside the country. Then, with the help of local villagers, he would search out little-known border crossings or mountain passes through which Bibles could be transported. Before long all twenty-five thousand of the little red New Testaments had been delivered by nomads or traders or relatives of believers in China.

David also encouraged Chinese Christians all over Asia to visit their country and find other believers, whether blood relatives or relatives in Christ. From the stories they brought back, David began to develop a clearer picture of the state of the Chinese church.

During the 1950s and 1960s, the church in China had been divided into two parts, official and unofficial. The official churches belonged to the government-sponsored Three-Self Patriotic Movement (self-government, self-support, self-propagation), which in practice meant that they agreed to cooperate with all regulations and limitations the government deemed necessary. Evangelism and the teaching of religion to children were strictly forbidden, and pastors were not allowed to preach on topics such as tithing (might affect the economy), healing, Sunday as a day of rest (the Chinese work seven days a week), and the second coming of Christ (might undermine people's commitment to the current regime). Three-Self policies also required the pastor and everyone in the church to register, making it easy for them to be tracked down if they stepped out of line. Undoubtedly there were (and are) genuine Christians among the members of Three-Self churches, but the faith they were allowed to practice inevitably required some degree of compromise.

For the most part, any church that had refused to become a Three-Self church during that period was shut down by the government. That included virtually all independent Protestant churches, most of which were strongly evangelical. Although some of the congregations dissolved, many continued to meet covertly in people's homes. Sometimes only one family or a few families would worship God together. In some areas larger groups of thirty, forty, even a hundred or more would gather in a believer's home at an odd hour, perhaps a weekday afternoon or in the middle of the night, singing quietly and listening to a pastor teach from the Word of God.

Such meetings were illegal, however, so many church leaders were persecuted and imprisoned. Pastor Wang Ming-Tao and Watchman Nee, two giants of the faith, remained in jail for years after their original sentences had expired. Mama Kwang, a fearless woman of God who conducted many house gatherings, had been to prison three times. Others were sent to labor camps. In 1966, when Mao launched the Cultural Revolution, his Red Guards swept across the country in an attempt to stamp out all religion. House churches endured a new wave of persecution, and even the Three-Self churches were completely closed down, forcing all Christians to go underground.

What effect did this brutal oppression have on the church? David was amazed to discover that the number of Christians had actually *grown* during that period, and at an incredible rate. In the mid-seventies, the number of believers was estimated to be in the tens of millions. (Today that estimate has grown to sixty million.) So David's vision for ten million Bibles wasn't at all unrealistic; if anything, it was too small!

—◄o►—

As more information came in about the needs of the Chinese church, I knew it was time to sponsor a conference of people who cared about China in order to pray and share resources. So David and I made phone calls and wrote letters to Christian leaders and mission groups all over the world. Would they come together to consider the task of conveying the message of Christ to today's China?

The response was very enthusiastic, and many planned to attend. A few groups pressed for a strong anticommunist agenda, but I told them, "No, I can't do that. This conference is *for* Jesus, not against communism. Jesus must be our central focus." We had decided to call the conference Love China, because we knew that without love for the Chinese people, there would be no hope of reaching them for Christ.

After more than five years of prayer and preparation, with Brother David handling most of the organizational details, the Love China conference convened for five days in Manila in September 1975. More than 430 delegates from twenty-three countries gathered, representing fifteen denominations and fifty-five mission organizations. *Time* magazine correspondent David Aikman called it "the first full-scale gathering anywhere in the world of evangelicals concerned about the Christian witness in China since the Communist government gained power in 1949."

For each day of the conference, we had a variety of experts, all Christians, speaking on topics related to our task. Some explained the history of the church in China and the state of the church there today. Others analyzed the impact of China's religious policies and clarified the differences between the teachings of Marx, Lenin, Mao, and Christ. Chinese Christians who had recently been in the country reported on the believers they had met and the suffering they had to undergo for the sake of Jesus. We all took a hard look at our own ministries to determine what we were doing—and not doing—to support the Chinese church and further the spread of the gospel. And every evening we spent time in prayer for that great country, its nine hundred million people (then), and its struggling but thriving fellowship of believers.

Early on I was able to speak and challenge everyone to take the offensive against the forces of evil in China. "I have to make one thing very clear tonight," I said. "The kingdom of God is not a reality and it is not understood and not believed and preached as long as we accept the status quo, the status quo of political and nationalistic frontiers. . . . Organizations and missions that explicitly state that they only work in countries where this is legal are missing the boat in this end time. Soon, it will not be legal anywhere in the world. . . .

"By faith in Christ and by prayer to God, by obedience to the Holy Spirit, by courage, by determination, and by supreme sacrifice we can accomplish the task of evangelizing China in our generation. But we'd better hurry. We've got to begin somewhere, but begin we must. And the answer is obvious: *We have to live a life that is more revolutionary than that of the revolutionaries.*"

Dr. Samuel Moffatt, a missionary in Korea at the time, echoed some of my thoughts. He quoted Jesus' words in Matthew 5:20: "Unless your righteousness surpasses that of the Pharisees and the teachers of the law, you will certainly not enter the kingdom of heaven." Then he said to us, "The Chinese communists have outdisciplined us, outworked us, and outcommitted us. Unless we are willing to match their commitment in our service for the Lord, we are never going to make a difference there."

I had a fabulous time sharing and praying with the Christian leaders. It was truly an inspiring group. But as each day passed, I felt a growing sense of frustration. Many of the delegates seemed to be resigned to the fact that China was closed and that little could be done. "We must simply accept that it is the will of God," some would say. Or to justify their inactivity, others would say, "We can only wait for God's timing; his train is never late."

I have found this to be a common attitude. But we are nowhere in Scripture called to automatically accept every circumstance in the world as God's will. Instead, we need to *resist* the forces of evil, to engage in spiritual warfare. Finally I stood and asked to make a few statements.

"I agree with you that God's timing is correct and that his train is always on time," I said. "But you are using an outdated train directory—and you've missed the train!"

No one seemed to get the message. But then, as the conference was winding down, a dear brother by the name of William Willis got up to speak. An older Welshman who had been converted in a great revival there in 1904, this man of God captivated us all with his message. I have never in my life seen a prayer warrior like this man. His topic was intercessory prayer.

Brother Willis preached on several key passages. One was Ezekiel 22:30–31: "I looked for a man among them who would build up the wall and stand before me in the gap on behalf of the land so I would not have to destroy it, but I found none. So I will pour out my wrath on them and consume them with my fiery anger, bringing down on their own heads all they have done, declares the Sovereign Lord." God was looking for people who would do more than pray, he explained. God wanted men and women who would *intercede* or "stand in the gap" for his people.

The other passage was the account of Moses and the golden calf in Exodus 32:30–32. After confronting the Israelites about their terrible sin, Moses went before the Lord to beg forgiveness on behalf of the people. So great were his love and concern for them that he said to the Lord, "Please forgive their sin—but if not, *then blot me out of the book you have written*" (emphasis added). That, Brother Willis emphasized, was true intercession. Were we willing to intercede for the people of China in that way?

By the time Brother Willis finished speaking, we had all fallen to our knees, praying, shedding tears, and interceding for the people of China and for one another. The Holy Spirit had broken down our defenses, and our entire attitude toward China changed. The spirit of resistance had returned, the spirit of prayer and intercession that made it possible to ignore human borders and political systems where the Christian faith is concerned.

I believe that night was a turning point not only for our ministry, but for all of China.

Why?

Within just one year of that conference, China experienced more upheaval than anyone could have imagined. First, Premier Chou En-lai died, causing much political instability as a power struggle ensued over who would succeed him.

Then the country was further destabilized as a powerful earthquake rocked northeast China, completely destroying one city of more than a million inhabitants and causing significant damage in Beijing. Though no official numbers were ever released, observers estimated that more than five hundred thousand people were killed.

Yet that was only the beginning. In September of 1976, Chairman Mao himself died. And shortly thereafter, the notorious Gang of Four, who represented the most radical and repressive elements of the government, were arrested.

All of those changes in just one year! As a result, China's brutal policies toward religious activity relaxed somewhat, its borders became more penetrable, and its people became more hungry than ever for the gospel. Certainly none of us at that Love China conference could claim any credit for it, but I have no doubt that God honored the concentrated intercessory prayers of all who participated.

By the end of 1976, Brother David and others of his team had already gone to China with small supplies of Bibles for the house churches. He gained the immediate trust of the Chinese believers by first asking them, "How is the body of Christ?" It reminded me so much of my own approach in the early years, when I would echo the words of Joseph, "I seek my brothers."

In early 1977, I joined David on another trip there, passing through customs with no difficulty at all. Thus began a program of Bible deliveries, training, and encouragement for the Chinese church that continues to this day. I could hardly believe how much had changed since my last visit eleven years earlier. The door was not only open—it had fallen off the hinges!

Step Four

─◀o▶─

Prepare to live as a Christian full time.

What's the difference between a hero and a coward? Both are ordinary people, both are scared, and both are running. But the hero is running in the right direction. Some kind of preparation took place that enabled him to act heroically.

The same is true for those of us whom God calls through his written Word. We, too, need to be prepared for his service. But before I explain some of the ways we can prepare, let me clarify what I mean by the calling of God.

In some evangelical circles, shortly after people commit their lives to Christ, they are confronted with a series of follow-up questions that sound something like this: "Has God chosen you to play a special role in his plan for the world? Do you have the gift of evangelism or preaching or teaching? In short, has God called you to full-time Christian service?"

These are not bad questions, but all too often they foster an attitude of categorizing Christians into two groups—the special few who are called, and then the rest of us who are merely Christians, but nothing special. Those who are called will do the evangelism, the preaching, and the missionary work, and those who aren't will simply look forward to being in heaven one day.

I am afraid this is the *opposite* of what it means to be called. There are no first-class or second-class Christians; one believer is no more special to God than another. The fact is, God calls *all* of us to full-time Christian service—that is, we are all called to be Christians full time. We may not pastor a church or go to Outer Mongolia, but in God's eyes we are just as much a part of the Great Commission as pastors and missionaries.

The real calling of God is not to a certain place or career, but to everyday obedience. And that call is extended to *every* Christian, not a select few. Then, as we follow his everyday call, he opens doors to where he wants us to go, and closes doors to where he does not want us to go. That way, faithfulness to God's calling is within our reach every day, and life becomes an adventure as we obey his Word and walk through the doors he has opened for us.

On the other hand, if we agonize over whether we have received a special call, we waste valuable time and energy and, in effect, limit the work of God in our lives. When people ask me whether they should go into full-time ministry in the traditional sense, I almost always discourage them. I tell them to follow Jesus with their whole lives and pursue full-time ministry only as a last resort.

How do we prepare to respond to that call? Part of the preparation is God's doing, and part of it must be ours. God's preparation of us began long before we decided to accept his call—long before we even knew who Christ was. The fact is, God has been using all of the events and experiences of our lives to prepare us for the kind of service he's calling us to now. Whether our past was happy or sad, godly or sordid, God is building on that experience to make us into effective servants for him.

It may take an entire lifetime of preparation for one minute of supreme service. In the case of John the Baptist, God used his whole life to prepare him for the moment when he saw the lone figure of Jesus approaching in the desert. He stopped baptizing and teaching, pointed his finger, and said, "Look, the Lamb of God, who takes away the sin of the world!" (John 1:29). What an electrifying moment in history, the first time Jesus was introduced to the world as the Lamb of God.

And yet look at the preparation John underwent. The way he dressed, the way he lived, the way he was treated. The barren desert he endured by day, and the cave he probably slept in at night. The restaurants he went to where they served only locusts with a side of honey. The confrontations he had with the religious leaders, the soldiers, and the tax collectors. The stern moral teaching that appeared to be more demanding and yet more freeing than the Jewish code. All that preparation brought John to that one climactic moment.

Or take Saul before he became Paul. He was a zealous Pharisee, totally committed to the persecution and murder of Christians. His vast knowledge of the Law and his absolute singleness of purpose were known throughout the land. God allowed that knowledge and zeal to develop so that one day Saul would be prepared to do God's work.

When I was growing up, I would never have dreamed that my experiences would be preparing me for the work I have now. I played nasty pranks on people and caused trouble as a kid. When the Nazi troops occupied Holland during World War II, I ran messages and interference for the Dutch Resistance, and did anything else I could to harass the soldiers. As the war progressed and our electricity and food were cut off, I learned to live on next to nothing. At one point the only food my parents could give us was a handful of tulip bulbs, which we cut into small slices to make them last for several days.

Looking back, I see how God used every one of those events to prepare me for his service. The dire conditions we lived under during the war helped me to identify with the hardships many Christian families face in repressive countries. And there are many more ways God prepared me. It's important that we not despise our own life experiences. We can look back and know that God will use them all for his service.

But there is another kind of preparation that is *our* responsibility. In Acts 20:28, Paul says, "Take heed therefore unto yourselves" (KJV). That means we are responsible for the spiritual state in which we live. We are responsible to work with this Word of God as he has given it to us. We are privileged people in this world: All of us have the Bible in our own language. All of us have enough intellect to read and understand. All of us have the desire to learn more of God. And all of us have everyday opportunities to worship and pray unhindered.

Paul goes on to say that we should take heed "to all the flock." We cannot possibly take heed to the flock of God unless we first take heed to ourselves. When we offer ourselves in service to the suffering church, will we have something to give them? Jesus constantly gave of himself during his ministry. When people touched him, power went out of him. That is why he got tired. So he took time each day, early in the morning, to get away from people and be alone with God, where he could be renewed and refreshed.

I truly need your prayers in this area. With all of my speaking and writing and traveling, I have sometimes failed to give myself enough time alone with God and his Word. Back in 1971, when I lay in the hospital after that plane crash, Corry sat at my bedside and read me the Scriptures for hours on end, day after day. I quickly realized how badly I needed that time to feed on the

Word of God. I had been doing too much, going too fast, and not replenishing my spiritual resources.

Jesus Christ has given us the awesome responsibility of feeding his church and sharing his message with the world. Unfortunately I see few Christians who take this challenge seriously. To live as a true member of Christ's church is not a hobby or something to do in spare time. It is very life! God does not work with volunteers. He *calls* us. Not one of the twelve apostles was a volunteer. Jesus called each of them and they left everything behind for him.

Just because God calls everyone does not mean we should take his call lightly. It is not easy to serve Jesus Christ full time. In fact, it is a *hard* life, but a very satisfying one. It means always being available for other people while completely giving up all rights to ourselves. It means allowing God to gradually make us into the persons he wants us to be so that everything we do arises out of who we are as Christians.

Are we ready to take on the biggest challenge in the world? Only if we prepare ourselves as individuals and as churches. The preparation must first take place within as we draw closer to the Lord and his teachings and grow in spiritual maturity. Then we will have the greatest impact when we reach out to our needy brothers and sisters around the world.

Formal education may play a part in our preparation, but not necessarily for all of us—myself included. I had almost no schooling beyond junior high, and when I attended the WEC missionary training school, the principal would later describe me as a very mediocre student. I'm not knocking education at all; I just don't want people to use it as an excuse to avoid or postpone doing what God wants them to do.

We have seen that there are many components to preparation. Our goal is to anticipate as many situations to prepare for as we can without neglecting to do the work itself. I have a close Russian friend who now lives in the West. Very soon after the Iron

Curtain fell and Russia opened up, he conducted a big evangelistic campaign in Moscow. In just a few days, *twelve thousand*
people made a decision to accept Jesus Christ. But after the
campaign ended, he spoke to me.

"Andrew, I will never do this again," he said tearfully. "All
these people came forward, and we had no Bibles to give them,
no one to pray with them, no one to follow up with them. I feel
guilty because we were not ready."

I foresee many more great opportunities for harvest around
the world. But are we ready? Are our churches ready? Are our
missions ready?

PRAYER

Lord, make me the proper tool in your hand.
Cause me to grow in my relationship with you so that when
opportunities arise to reap your harvest,
I will be completely prepared.
Amen.

Chapter Five

—◄○►—

It Will Never Happen Here!

There are two kinds of people in the world—those who say about persecution, "It will never happen here!" and those who say, "I *thought* it would never happen here!"

The saddest experience is meeting people who used to belong to the first group, but now belong to the second. Looking back, they can recognize that the signs of impending persecution were present, but for some reason they didn't prepare for it. Perhaps they allowed their faith to become complacent or they were seduced by materialism or they refused to believe that conditions were changing in their country.

For example, a colleague who used to work as a missionary in Vietnam told me that only days before Da Nang fell to the Viet Cong in April 1975, some South Vietnamese pastors were at a conference mulling over a ten-year plan for the church, assuming business would continue as usual. They seemed unaware that their "free" country was crumbling around them! Instead of working to prepare Christians for life under persecution, they were talking about church building programs.

At about that time I noticed that the revolution was moving to a new frontier: Africa. Russia and China were eager to take advantage of the economic instability and political unrest there. By identifying young intellectuals and giving them a free education—in other words, Marxist indoctrination—they hoped to create a strong communist presence in Africa. In addition, they would send money and arms to various "liberation" movements in exchange for their allegiance. Eventually they hoped to control the continent with its vast supply of workers and natural resources.

Among the first African countries to come under Marxist influence were Angola, Mozambique, South-West Africa (now Namibia), Uganda, and others. Sure enough, the very same things I saw happen in Eastern Europe and in Cuba were happening there. Missionaries were thrown into jail. Churches were closed or meeting times restricted. Bible publishing was shut down. In Uganda, Idi Amin's ruthless regime imprisoned and murdered thousands of Christians, and the Marxist government of Equatorial Guinea slaughtered Catholics by the thousands and turned their churches into warehouses. In South Africa, growing racial tensions caused by apartheid had nearly reached the breaking point, and with communism on the rise in nearby countries, the people were nervous about their own nation's security.

The church in Africa needed to prepare for the sweeping revolution, to learn how to stand firm amid persecution. I felt strongly that the evangelical church in South Africa should lead the way for the rest of the continent. With all its flaws, it remained the most stable and mature body of believers in Africa, and it had the most resources. So, working with my contacts in the Hospital Christian Fellowship in South Africa, I traveled there and held meetings around the country.

Whether I spoke in the mostly white, bustling city of Johannesburg or in the sprawling black shantytowns, I insisted that all meetings be integrated. I would not accept an invitation from or speak in a facility that forbade any race or class from attending. In many cases that proved to be more of a symbolic gesture than a reality, given the political tensions, but at least I made it clear that everyone was welcome.

The people of South Africa were fascinated by my stories of smuggling Bibles to suffering Christians behind the Iron Curtain. One group even sat down with me and said they wanted to help me take Bibles to Russia. I realized they were missing my point entirely.

"Do you have servants—black servants?" I asked.

Yes, they replied.

"Have you given Bibles to your servants and shared your faith with them?"

Well, no, not really, they said, and made a few excuses about why.

"Listen," I said, probably too strongly, "I don't want your help with Russian Bibles when I know you're neglecting a great need right under your noses. Your first responsibility as a Christian is to South Africa, and then to all of the African continent."

The same is true for all of us. It's useless to think we can make a difference for Christ in some remote corner of the world if we can't do it in our own neighborhoods, schools, and workplaces. I wanted my South African brothers and sisters to start with their own country and branch out from there.

I also warned them that it would be no simple task to build up the church amid the growing clashes between apartheid, communism, dictatorships, and tribal warfare. They could no longer stick their heads in the sand and hope Africa's problems would go away. It was time to step out, to act, and to be ready to pay the price of suffering.

"As white South Africans, are you willing to be sold as slaves to black Africans in order to spread the gospel?" I would challenge them. Would they be willing to accept a complete reversal of that evil system of apartheid if that was the only way to bring Christ to the rest of Africa? I admit I was hard on them, but many responded with tremendous dedication.

The young people especially impressed me. On one of my visits I worked with some of the Youth with a Mission (YWAM) leaders and spoke to high schools and universities throughout South Africa. The students were so willing to respond, even to lay their lives on the line for the cause of Christ. Out of that one speaking tour came a YWAM training school that is still operating today. It served as a vivid reminder to me that our young people are such a wonderful and valuable resource for the kingdom—then and now. We must always pray for them and challenge them to do great things for God.

By the mid-1970s we had established an Open Doors base in South Africa. An elderly Dutch Reformed pastor, Koos Driescher, offered himself as our first full-time worker. Our next task was to reach out to the other African countries and find out what the church needed. So my colleagues and I began to travel extensively throughout Zambia, Rhodesia, Malawi, and other southern African countries and meet with Christian leaders. Since we had recently had a successful Love China conference, we decided to explore the possibility of a Love Africa conference as well.

In our travels we made many wonderful friends and had rich times of fellowship. And wherever we went, we saw similar patterns. There was a tremendous openness to Christ among Africans. We spoke in large, rapidly growing churches of all denominations and received a warm response. But we also noticed that many of the churches were not well grounded in Scripture. Some had allowed their faith to become watered down by prevailing political winds, while others had combined it with tribal superstitions. We saw a vast need for sound teaching among the Christians.

In most of the African countries, the other piece of the puzzle was persecution. It always seemed to be increasing or just on the horizon. We spent many days and weeks on our knees with the believers, praying that God would keep them strong in the difficult days to come.

—◄○►—

Meanwhile, I continued to travel to Africa's ever-increasing crisis areas to offer help and encouragement to the Christians. I visited Uganda several times during Idi Amin's reign of terror. The dictator himself was a militant Muslim of the Kakwa tribe. Early on I met with the Anglican archbishop of the country, Janani Luwum. A devoted follower of Christ, he was in an extremely difficult position. He was not only head of the Church of Uganda, but also head chaplain of Amin's military. It wasn't long before he began to fear for his life.

Archbishop Luwum and I became good friends, and in the fall of 1976 I asked how I could help him in his vital work. One area of need was Bibles for the Ugandan soldiers. Chaplains had been sharing Christ among the men, but they had almost no Bibles to give out. So I sent out an appeal to Open Doors supporters, and within a few months we had shipped fifty thousand Bibles to Uganda—one for nearly every serviceman.

Unfortunately conditions worsened dramatically the following year. Amin moved forcibly to set up a Muslim state in a country that was 60 percent Christian. Anyone who voiced even the slightest opposition to Amin or government policies was reported and usually executed. Thousands met their death at the hands of his army or his brutal secret police force, who would arrest or kill people without warning.

As more and more Christians vanished, the archbishop knew he could not be silent. He began to speak out against the atrocities, and he personally pleaded with Amin to stop. After he delivered a letter of protest to Amin signed by eighteen Ugandan bishops, the dictator ordered the archbishop arrested and executed. According to reports, the soldiers refused to kill him, however, so Amin pulled out his own gun and murdered the archbishop himself—by shooting him through the mouth.

Grief-stricken at the loss of this courageous brother and of the thousands of other Christians executed in the weeks that followed, I determined to go back to Uganda to stand with the believers. They had already held an unofficial memorial service in the great Namirembe Cathedral in Kampala, but on June 30, 1977, another important ceremony was to take place there—a celebration of the one hundredth anniversary of the Anglican church in Uganda. Services like that, as well as regular Sunday services, were permitted, but Christians placed themselves at great personal risk by attending.

I arranged for my colleagues, Jan and Johan, to fly with me into Kampala. It was an extremely dangerous time to enter the country because Amin's tidal wave of persecution was at its height. The situation was further complicated by Israel's recent bombing of Entebbe Airport in Kampala after one of its planes had been hijacked. Security would be very tight.

As our plane circled to land at Entebbe, I was horrified at the sight of the airport below. The carcasses of many MIG fighter jets destroyed in the Israeli raid still remained on the runways. No one had found time to clean up the wreckage. Bomb craters littered the rest of the landscape. Our plane touched down, and we taxied past bombed-out hangars and buildings pocked with bullet holes. We all sat frozen in our seats.

Once we arrived at the gate, I expected people to get up and start collecting their bags to leave the plane. But no one moved. After an awkward silence, the flight attendant finally announced,

"Will the three men who are deplaning here please come forward?"

We were the only ones getting off! Everyone else was continuing to another destination. And as far as they were concerned, the plane couldn't take off too soon. They all looked at us like we were crazy. I wondered for a moment whether we were.

The relatively new and modern terminal was nearly deserted except for the ever-watchful police, who easily outnumbered the passengers. Our footsteps echoed eerily as we proceeded to customs. We had brought only our personal Bibles on this trip, so I didn't have to worry about being searched. The officials did confiscate my copy of *Time* magazine, however.

With public transportation in Kampala ground to a virtual halt, we had to find a creative way to get to our hotel and then to the various contacts we had made. Cars carrying foreigners were routinely followed or stopped, and often robbed by the police. But my friends in Hospital Christian Fellowship had arranged to transport us around the city in the one vehicle that was never stopped or searched—an ambulance. It came in extremely handy on several occasions when we needed to get through roadblocks or checkpoints.

On Sunday we attended the centenary service at the marvelous red brick cathedral on Namirembe Hill, the Hill of Peace. Jan, Johan, and I were almost the only white faces in the crowded sanctuary. In spite of the high anxiety in the air, the worship was fervent and full. Silvanus Wani, the new archbishop, led the liturgy and spoke of the "martyr who died for the nation," though he did not mention Janani Luwum by name. There was no need. Everyone present—including the hundreds of bystanders outside the church listening over loudspeakers—knew exactly who he was talking about.

I had spoken with several of Idi Amin's aides earlier in hopes of arranging a private meeting. We had actually set a specific appointment time, but later that day, it was abruptly canceled.

The official reason? The dictator had suddenly decided to confer upon himself an additional title: Conqueror of the British Empire. So he had sent people scurrying about to arrange a lavish ceremony.

Meanwhile, Jan, Johan, and I snooped around the Kampala area for the next few days, meeting with Christian leaders and joining in with several secret worship gatherings. I was deeply moved by the believers' level of commitment and their lack of fear in the face of so much suffering. Many of them had friends and family members who for no other reason than their Christian faith had been hauled away to prison or to their death.

Idi Amin's not-so-secret police were responsible for most of the impromptu arrests. Known officially as members of the State Research Bureau, the Gestapolike men wore dark glasses, flower-patterned shirts, bell-bottoms, and platform shoes, and they usually drove around the city in white Range Rovers.

I noticed them hanging around the Kampala International Hotel where we were staying. Even though it was probably the safest hotel in the city, it was far from secure. Phones frequently did not work, and power outages were common. Even food was scarce. Often we were unable to get a cup of coffee, and on the few occasions that we did, there was no milk or sugar. And this at an international hotel.

The nights were full of action, too. After a busy day of encouraging our Ugandan brothers and sisters, we had returned to the hotel, exhausted. We locked ourselves in our separate rooms, and I immediately sank into a sound sleep. Jan and Johan also went to bed.

During the middle of the night, Johan was jolted awake by the sound of screaming. Some kind of scuffle was taking place on the floor above. He ran to the window and looked down. Sure enough, several white Range Rovers were parked outside. Then there was more screaming, more people running up and down the hall. Amin's police were barging into people's rooms and dragging them away!

Absolutely terrified, Johan grabbed his things and ducked into Jan's room, where they sat up the rest of the night and, with hearts pounding, prayed for our safety. The rascals never bothered to warn me, but it was just as well—I slept through the whole thing. The incident made us more aware of what it must be like for Christians who live there every day. At any moment, day or night, they could be ambushed by those henchmen.

When Jan and Johan told me the next morning what had happened, I knew we were in danger. It would be only a matter of time before the police would come after us, too. We slipped out of the hotel and made it to another meeting where I had been asked to preach. Afterward, one of the Christian leaders confirmed my suspicions.

"Yes, we've heard that the police know what you're doing here," he said. "It's very dangerous for you to stay any longer. If I were you, I'd take the next flight out of the country. Don't even go back to your hotel."

Fortunately we had brought our luggage with us. So we said a hasty good-bye and climbed back into the ambulance to go straight to the airport. At the entrance to Entebbe Airport, the police inspectors again let us pass right through.

We had arrived well before that day's departure time, but we needed standby seats to Nairobi, so we waited at the ticket counter for an agent. As the line grew longer and longer behind us, I feared that the flight would be full and we'd be left behind. After all, many people besides us were eager to leave the terror-ridden country.

I also worried that if the flight was delayed, the police would catch up with us right there at the airport. As sort of a security measure, I had bought a large portrait of Idi Amin that I carried under my arm, so it could be easily seen. If the police saw me with his picture, perhaps they wouldn't arrest me. The three of us prayed silently for God's intervention and reminded each other that friends of Open Doors around the world were praying for us.

Finally the woman who handled the ticketing arrived. We held our breath as she made an announcement.

"Ladies and gentlemen," she said, "I'm afraid we have a problem. All of our computers are down, and we do not have a copy of the passenger list for this flight. So I will allow those who got here first to board the plane first, starting at the front of the line."

The flight was completely full. But we were among the very first passengers to board.

When we finally got back to Holland, we received word from the believers in Uganda that the secret police had indeed been waiting for us at the Kampala International Hotel. It had been the closest call of my entire ministry—so far.

Several years later, after the Tanzanian army had driven Idi Amin into exile, Jan returned to Uganda to determine how we at Open Doors could help the church get back on its feet. One of the stops he made was at the notorious State Research Bureau's former headquarters in Nakasero, which lay in ruins. Literally thousands of executions had been performed there, and blood stains still covered the floors of the interrogation rooms.

In one office, Jan noticed a stack of files and notebooks that had been dumped on the floor, and he began picking through them. They turned out to be long lists of names, people whom the police were supposed to round up for questioning, torture, or worse. He glanced through some of the notebooks, hardly believing that one man could have waged such a campaign of death. Some have estimated that Idi Amin ordered between five hundred thousand and eight hundred thousand deaths during his reign.

But then something caught Jan's eye. Looking closer at one of the pages, his jaw dropped and a shiver ran down his spine.

There on Amin's execution list was his own name, along with mine.

Meanwhile, the Tanzanian soldier accompanying Jan was growing impatient and wanted him to drop everything and leave.

Jan looked up at him and said, "Would you want your name to be in this book?"

"Noooo," the soldier replied, his face growing fearful.

"Well, neither do I," Jan said, and he tore out the page. I still have it in my files.

-◄o►-

It amazes me how God leads the way when you get up and go to his people around the world. He always seems to guide you to the right people and the right situations. Often, I have found, the guidance does not happen until after I've left for where I'm going. Of course, I plan my itinerary, but I also listen for the Spirit's leading, pay close attention to the people I bump into, and remain open to changing my plans and seizing a God-given opportunity. Let me give an example.

I had been invited to preach in a number of churches in Angola, which at that time was embroiled in a civil war. The de facto communist government, known as the Popular Movement for the Liberation of Angola (MPLA), controlled the northern part of the country from the capital city of Luanda. The MPLA was funded and supported by the USSR and Cuba. Two other guerrilla groups, the National Front for the Liberation of Angola (FNLA) and the Union for the Total Independence of Angola (UNITA), operated primarily in the south. The FNLA looked to the U.S. Central Intelligence Agency and China for backing, and UNITA relied on South Africa.

As always, my purpose in visiting was not to fight against any political group, but to strengthen the church and share the Bible with believers and anyone else who hungered for spiritual truth. If possible, I also hoped to share the Christian message with members of the warring factions so they might seek a peaceful resolution to the conflict.

From Holland I first had to fly to Paris in order to get a flight into Angola. The man sitting next to me turned out to be an executive with Heineken, the Dutch beer company. He knew about the situation in Angola because Heineken had a plant there. We talked about the awful conditions, so many people fighting and dying, and so many fleeing the country.

"You know," he said, "we have never left the country."

Hmm, I thought. I find it interesting that on many occasions when a communist or military regime takes over a country, everyone rushes to leave, but big business stays in. If business can remain, why don't Christians and missions groups? Are we simply unwilling to take the risk?

At the airport transfer desk in Paris, I stood next to a black gentleman who looked at me very intently.

"Sir, I think I know you from somewhere," he said.

"I really don't know," I said. "Where are you from?"

He turned out to be an official in the provisional government of Namibia. We didn't know each other, but we were getting on the same plane and going to the same place. During the flight, I walked over to his seat and continued the conversation. We talked a lot about Idi Amin, the situation in southern Africa and the changes sweeping across the continent. When we were finished, he invited me to visit their government base. They also had a military base, he explained, and I knew that both were connected with the guerrilla warfare they had been and still were engaged in.

When our plane arrived at the airport in Luanda, we saw hundreds of displaced people sleeping outside. Many of them had plane tickets in hand to leave the country, but their flights never came. The city had no public transportation because there were no spare parts to keep the buses running. The shelves of grocery stores and other shops were empty because the production of food and other goods had ground to a halt. As in Uganda, the International Hotel was the only decent facility I could stay in, mainly because members of the international press stay there. It was also the only place I could buy a cup of coffee.

We had some tremendous church services in the north, where Christians were alternately harassed and disregarded by the MPLA. A drama presentation by one congregation perfectly captured their precarious situation and their hope in God. They had built a "fiery furnace" in one corner of the church, and several adults and children reenacted the events of the Daniel story. A raging Nebuchadnezzar had ordered three faithful believers to be cast into the inferno because they refused to bow down before his man-made god. As three of the actors were thrust into the furnace, real smoke poured forth from the opening and spread all over the church. Then, moments later, *four* actors emerged victoriously from the oven amid wild applause and shouts of hallelujah from the congregation. What a beautiful introduction to the message I was about to present to them.

Later on during that trip, I went to the government base to see the official I'd met on the plane. He introduced me to some of the other ministers of state of the SWAPO movement, and we had an entire afternoon of stimulating, even enjoyable conversation. I made it absolutely clear that I was coming to them in the name of Christ. The men were Marxists, liberation fighters, and no doubt they had either killed many people or ordered others to kill. Yet they seemed interested in the simple truth of the gospel.

"Listen," I said at one point. "There is one thing I don't like about your offices here."

"What is it?" they said.

"Well, on every desk I see a bust of Lenin," I replied.

"So what are you asking us to do?" they said.

"I want you to give your people a choice. Lenin is not the only message in the world. There is an alternative and his name is Jesus. Give your people the opportunity to choose. Surely no nation can be happy when its people are forced to live under a system that they have not chosen—be it political or religious. I want you to let me place a Bible on the desk next to Lenin. Then, when people come into your headquarters, they see you are fair —you can have either Lenin or Jesus."

To my amazement, they liked my idea. So I took out some Bibles I had brought in their language, and I put one next to the bust of Lenin.

That entire experience with the guerrilla leaders came about because a black African whom I'd never seen before struck up a conversation with me in an airport. Who could have orchestrated such an encounter but the Lord? Of course, recognizing such a moment was not enough; I also needed to follow up with him and be willing to change my plans.

On my next visit to Angola, I went to the south, where much of the guerrilla activity took place. It was too dangerous to travel there from the north, so I had to start in South Africa and then fly to the Caprivi strip, which borders Angola on the south. Because the South African military was backing the UNITA rebels in southern Angola, the South Africans were more than happy to help Jan Pit and me get across the border to meet some of them.

They sneaked us in by helicopter, flying at treetop level to avoid radar detection. We had no traveling papers with us—only Bibles. We landed in what seemed like the middle of nowhere and found hundreds of guerrilla soldiers, many of whom identified themselves as Christians. So we held several large meetings right there in the bush country. They treated us like dignitaries.

I had several long talks with the leader of the UNITA movement, Jonas Savimbi. He comes from a Presbyterian background, and was eager to pray and even sing gospel hymns with us. I urged him to stop the killing and search for a peaceful solution to his country's problems. I am sad to report that my advice fell on deaf ears because even today he is carrying on the same kind of violent warfare.

We found many other Christians in the area, both Catholic and Protestant. At a Communion service we conducted in a very primitive church building, so many people tried to get in that the soldiers had to keep the surging crowd away at gunpoint. Since that visit our Open Doors teams have gone back to give them Scriptures, child evangelism materials, and training seminars.

◄o►

During our travels around Africa, I had both uplifting and heartbreaking experiences, often at the same time. Many groups I preached to lived in absolute poverty—annual income of only a few hundred dollars—and yet they glowed with the joy of knowing Christ. At one Christian camp in Rwanda, one of the poorest countries in all of Africa, the young people were so moved by the story I told about imprisoned Russian pastor Georgi Vins that they took up an offering for me to give to his family. That broke my heart.

On another occasion, I spoke about Christ in a squalid prison where hundreds of men were packed into one open room with a muddy floor and a single toilet hole in the corner. Many of the prisoners had committed no crime but had been locked up solely because of their political views. Yet I was overwhelmed by their remarkable openness to Jesus.

In Tanzania, I learned of a great need for the Scriptures among the tens of thousands of Chinese workers who had been imported to build the Tan-Zam Railway. I remembered the Chinese New Testaments I had worked on earlier with Brother David, the ones that looked like Mao's Red Book. They would be the perfect thing to give to the displaced laborers. Quickly we went back to press and delivered fifty thousand copies to the labor camps.

In each country I visited, I would seek the Christian leaders and find out the church's greatest needs. I also asked if they'd be willing to gather with other African Christian leaders and evangelical missions organizations to pray for their continent and consider how they could work together to strengthen the church.

The conference finally came together in Malawi in 1978. We called it Love Africa, in the same vein as Love China three years earlier. In attendance were 250 delegates from thirty-seven African countries south of the Sahara. (Since all the countries north of the Sahara were predominantly Muslim, we decided to save them for a Love Muslims conference sometime in the future.) A variety of mission groups working in Africa also sent representatives.

Overall Love Africa went very well, and we had a rich time of prayer and fellowship. But the gathering was not without controversy. At one point, after a black bishop had recounted his experiences of discrimination under apartheid, a leading white South African theologian attempted to justify his country's policy of racial separation. Suddenly the emotionally charged issue of apartheid was threatening to break up the entire conference. Several groups were calling on each other to formally apologize, and others wanted me to announce an official position on the issue. Although I certainly disagreed with South Africa's policy of apartheid, it was not my place to take an official stance for or against it. I wanted to focus on the deeper spiritual issues.

It saddened me that those two groups failed to reconcile at the conference, but by the time it came to an end, a much greater sense of unity had prevailed. The unifying theme? Persecution. The church in nearly every African country either had it in some form or saw it coming. Unless the people of God would ground themselves in the Scriptures and support one another in prayer, they would not be able to stand firm.

One speaker in particular drove this point home. Gerhard Hamm, a well-known evangelist in Russia, spoke on what it means to suffer for one's faith and how Christ had given him the strength to endure. Brother Hamm knew from experience what he was talking about. His father had died in a Siberian prison for preaching the gospel, and Gerhard himself had spent many years in jail for his faith in Jesus. We at Open Doors had known about him during his imprisonment and had helped to support his family. When he was finally released and arrived in the West, we met him and offered him a full-time speaking position. Today he lives near Bonn, Germany, and though he is getting older, he continues to be very much involved in ministry. His son Victor travels and preaches throughout Siberia, and we provide him with Bibles and literature.

Brother Hamm told everyone what kind of suffering Christians will experience under a communist regime. Communism had just hit the shores of Africa at that time. To some it appeared to be a positive, sane alternative to apartheid and tribalism and military dictatorships. Gerhard opened their eyes to the stark reality behind the glowing facade.

Several things about his speech made an impact. For one, he is an emotional, riveting speaker, and the pain he and his family had to endure was dreadful. As I translated his broken German into English and then listened as it was translated into French, I saw tears in many people's eyes. But I believe another factor was that he was white. Black Africans rarely hear of white men going to prison. It's always other black people who go there, at the hands of whites or of other blacks. For them to hear a white man tell of the same kind of abuse and mistreatment they were used to receiving made a strong impression.

For some of the participants, Brother Hamm's message was painfully prophetic. Shortly after the conference, the Ethiopian government was overthrown by the communists, and within a year the Ethiopian delegates from our conference were imprisoned.

◄○►

Since Love Africa, Open Doors teams have been actively working with the church in Angola, Mozambique, Rwanda,

Somalia, South Africa (Soweto), Tanzania, Uganda, and Zambia. Scripture distribution is part of our ministry, but our primary task has been training for African ministers and Christian leaders.

In Mozambique, for example, we train hundreds of pastors each year at a special school where most of the teachers are fellow African ministers. Since many of the pastors who attend never had the opportunity to attend Bible college or seminary, we focus on teaching them solid scriptural truth, showing them how to study the Bible and how to develop their own spiritual, devotional, and prayer life. The name we have given to this work is Project Timothy, after the training the young disciple received from the apostle Paul.

At the same time, we prepare them for the reality of persecution with a little book we have put together known as the *Victory Manual.* In it we give many principles and illustrations drawn from the suffering church in Eastern Europe, Russia, and China. The book helps them to establish how close they are to experiencing persecution in their own country, and provides practical help and encouragement so they can remain strong in their faith.

The final paragraph of the manual says, "Thousands of Christians have stood in persecution, but tens of thousands have fallen. Even in the days of great Roman persecution, only a small fraction of those who had professed Christ stood true to the end. More Christians have suffered for their faith in the twentieth century than in any other time in church history. Why are some able to stand? Because they have learned how to sink their roots of faith deeply into the rock, Jesus Christ."

Step Five

◄○►

Penetrate every devil-inspired boundary or barrier.

In Open Doors we are probably best known for our efforts at penetrating closed borders—smuggling Scriptures, conducting secret training seminars, and meeting other needs of the suffering church. Penetration follows from the previous steps of prayer and preparation, but we then go one stage further by bringing or sending in the actual message of Christ.

This message can take many forms—Bibles, Christian literature, radio broadcasts, or personal visits, for example. We may do it on a small scale, such as carrying Bibles in our luggage, or a large scale, such as sending fifty thousand Bibles to soldiers in the Ugandan army. In one case, our 1981 penetration of Scriptures into China amounted to a full-scale invasion we called Project Pearl. And we want to penetrate not only closed countries but any devil-inspired, man-made barrier that excludes people from the message of Christ, including the racial, social, political, cultural, denominational, language, and other barriers we face in our schools and businesses.

Furthermore, the methods we use to penetrate may be legal or illegal according to the laws of the target country. Our first choice is always to find legal means to bring in the Christian message, but if there are none, or if they are so limiting that the church cannot fully function, then we must obey the higher law of God and penetrate by whatever means we can, including smuggling. My only caution is that we must not compromise the rest of Scripture in the name of "obeying God rather than man."

I have endured much criticism over the years for my position on smuggling. However, many of my critics see no problem with beaming Christian broadcasts into closed countries, even though that is just as illegal. Sometimes I wonder if people oppose smuggling ultimately because it involves more risk on our part than radio. (I might add that people on the receiving end can be arrested for listening to Christian broadcasts as well as for accepting Bibles.) But the most important issue for me is not whether we smuggle, but whether we go at all.

Going is what evangelism and missions—and penetration—are all about. You cannot spell the word *gospel* or even *God* without first spelling *go*. In 1 Thessalonians 1:5, the apostle Paul writes, "Our gospel came to you not simply with words, but also with power, with the Holy Spirit and with deep conviction." Notice the key phrase: Our gospel *came to you*. That's penetration—the fulfillment of Jesus' command, "Go into all the world." As I see it, those who stay behind need a clearer call than those who go.

We must take the initiative. We can't wait for the unsaved to come to us because then they will come not as friends, but as revolutionaries, occupation armies, or terrorists. The scriptural order is that we first go to them and *then* proclaim. When we do this, whether it be across closed borders or across the street, there will always be a confrontation. Why? Because the powers that be in a closed country or system or environment will never willingly accept us in to proclaim the message of Jesus Christ. However much people *need* the message, however much God wants us to be there, it will never happen without *our* paying the cost. That's why Paul says the gospel comes with power and with the Holy Spirit and with deep conviction. Penetration leads to confrontation, and God gives us the power we need to be strong in that confrontation.

A few years ago I visited with a group of Apache Indians in the U.S. They gave me the Apache name that means "he who crosses the lines." Not only do these words express one of our operating principles in Open Doors, but they should also define the calling of every Christian. If we truly want to spread the good news of Christ, we must penetrate into *all* the world—our neighborhoods, offices, schools, as well as regions across the globe. Not just where we are welcome or where the risk is minimal, but everywhere—*especially* the places where no other Christians have been.

PRAYER

Lord, help me to do something for you today
that I have never done before.
Amen.

Chapter Six

◄o►

Gabriella *and* Michael

*T*he Open Doors Asia staff and I were among the first to go
into China after an incredible spiritual breakthrough there. At
the Love China conference, we had heard plenty of reports and
statistics about Christians in China. But to experience the flourishing house-church movement firsthand was astounding. Instead of a small, discouraged, and beaten-down group of Christians, we found a huge network of millions of believers—strong,
principled, bold, courageous, and yes, persecuted.

One of them was a simple woman of God we affectionately
called Mama Kwang. Called by God at a young age to serve as
an evangelist, she traveled all over the south of China preaching,
teaching, and organizing house churches. Years before I had the
joy of meeting her, we had heard reports of hundreds, even thou-

sands, of people coming to Christ through her ministry, and many miraculous healings as well.

Because of her courageous witness, Mama Kwang was arrested and imprisoned on three occasions. But she kept right on sharing her faith with the other prisoners and the guards and led many of them to Christ. Each time she was released, she resumed her preaching and teaching the very next day. Similarly, her husband, a mathematics professor, had been sent to labor camps for many years. When they had both returned home from their last terms of punishment, Mrs. Kwang once again continued her ministry but remained in hiding much of the time to elude the authorities.

The house churches in southern China grew at an astonishing rate under her leadership. In the cities where police surveillance was tighter, groups ranging from three or four to as many as one hundred would gather secretly for prayer, worship, and teaching. But in the rural, outlying areas, it was not uncommon for a thousand or more believers to meet in one place. With so many new Christians, Mrs. Kwang saw the dramatic need for more Bibles. She sent an urgent request for one thousand Scriptures through one of Open Doors Asia's Chinese coworkers.

Up to that point Open Doors teams had never carried in more than forty or fifty Bibles at a time per team, so a delivery of that size represented a greater challenge and greater risk. But after much prayer and much planning, Brother David, his wife, and four Chinese Christians successfully carried in nine hundred Scriptures packed into their luggage. The final hundred came on a separate trip. Though it was much too dangerous for them to meet Mama Kwang during their courier visit, they later received word of how overjoyed she was for those copies of God's Word.

All of our Bible deliveries to China, large or small, came about in response to the requests of the Chinese church. We did not go there to impose our programs on them, but to learn how we could support their ministry. Whenever our Asia staff met with the Chinese Christians, they always tried to determine exactly what kinds of Scriptures were needed—complete Bibles or portions, adult or children's versions, which dialects, and so on. We even provided two forms of Chinese script—the older, traditional script still used today in Hong Kong and Taiwan, or the new simplified script introduced by Chairman Mao.

As Mrs. Kwang continued to teach and preach, she began to hear the Lord telling her that one day her family would leave the country to share the needs of the Chinese church with the rest of the world. Unfortunately getting out of the country was impossible by law for anyone who had been to prison. But that did not stop Mama and Papa Kwang from completing all the necessary visa applications and trusting God. For several years they received no reply. Then one morning in the spring of 1979, while Mrs. Kwang kneeled in prayer, she sensed God telling her that the family would leave China in one month.

Believing what she had heard, she immediately began to train the other leaders to carry on the ministry. No one in the family made any attempt to contact the authorities or check on the status of their applications. They knew God had spoken, and they planned for his will to happen, in spite of the doubts of some of the Christians. On the last day of the month, Mrs. Kwang prayed with all the leaders she had instructed, and she commissioned them to continue the work.

Sure enough, the very next day an official showed up at their door.

"Come with me," he said. "You are all to go to the police station. Your exit papers are waiting for you."

A day later the Kwangs arrived in Hong Kong, to everyone's surprise. Brother David, who had been in Hong Kong three days earlier to order thirty thousand New Testaments from the Bible Society, grabbed a flight from Manila and rushed back to greet them. He had never met them in person before, but they had communicated frequently and prayed for each other daily. And since David had carried a photo of the Kwang family in his wallet, he recognized them at once.

They embraced warmly amid tears of joy. Then Mrs. Kwang began to relate through an interpreter the story of their exit from China, and all the news from the believers inside. Brother David quickly realized that she had no intention of stopping her ministry now that she was free. She wanted to continue building up the Chinese church, and she sat down with David to develop a strategy. Unquestionably that would mean more Scriptures.

"How many Bibles do the believers need right now?" he asked her.

His jaw dropped as he listened to the interpreter's reply: "Brother David, she says they need thirty thousand Scriptures for the network leadership—immediately."

It was the exact number he had ordered only a few days earlier.

◄o►

Thus began the planning for Project Rainbow, our biggest Bible delivery attempt to China so far. How would we do it? The Asia team came up with a clever idea. The Canton Trade Fair would be taking place that October. Every spring and fall the significant event brought thousands of foreign businessmen by invitation to Canton for two weeks. Only groups were allowed into the country, but during their visit, they were treated better than tourists.

Our strategy was to ask Christian businessmen to request an invitation and then include other Christians in their group. That would make a volume delivery possible. Paul Estabrooks, who had just come from FEBC to join the Open Doors Asia staff, coordinated the travelers and trip logistics. Others were given responsibility for delivery of the Scriptures inside China, group briefings, and home-base operations.

The project plan was for thirty couriers—staff and friends of

Open Doors from around the world—to visit China during the Trade Fair. They were to bring two large empty suitcases and a shoulder bag with their clothing. In Hong Kong, each empty suitcase would be packed with five hundred of the mini-New Testaments, for a total of one thousand books per person. Thirty couriers, a thousand Bibles each, would add up to thirty thousand Bibles for the Chinese Christians.

To minimize suspicion, the couriers would enter China at various dates and times over the two-week period, usually in groups of three or four. The riskiest part of the task was going through customs, where bags were periodically (but not always) checked. We were especially vulnerable at that point because the suitcases would have nothing but Scriptures in them. If the official so much as opened one of the cases, that person's load would be immediately discovered.

Another factor was the sheer weight of the suitcases. As part of the briefing, the couriers were told that they needed to make their bags appear as light as feathers when they walked through customs. That was easier said than done for some on the team, which included a few older men, several women, and a young man with a broken foot. (Afterward, those who lugged those heavy suitcases referred to the operation not as Project Rainbow, but as Project Hernia.)

Finally in October the fair began, and so did our deliveries. Everything appeared to be going smoothly; several thousand New Testaments made it into China without a hitch. But then customs officials found two of our couriers' loads. The men were still allowed to enter, but they had to leave the books behind and pick them up when they left the country.

The project leaders were concerned. Their big question was, What do we do now? Were they on to us? Are the believers waiting for their delivery in danger? Should we shut down the operation? Everyone on the team decided to wait for twenty-four hours and pray. In Holland, after hearing about the potential problem, I called a meeting of our staff, and we spent considerable time in earnest prayer.

We all agreed the Lord was telling us to continue. The remaining couriers proceeded to go in. Several days later when the men whose loads had been discovered left China, they were permitted to take their Scriptures back to Hong Kong. There they were repacked into different suitcases and taken back in by someone else.

One courier had a particularly difficult time managing his heavy bags, and by the time he reached customs they seemed to weigh a ton each. So as he reached for his luggage to approach the official, he prayed, "In the name of Jesus, *rise.*" The bags seemed to lift right off the floor. He breezed through the customs check, and as soon as he made it around the corner, the bags crashed down again.

When it was over, thirty thousand New Testaments had safely reached the hands of grateful Chinese believers—all in a matter of days. We praised God for his faithfulness and his protection. Nothing was too difficult for him, no task too big.

-◄o►-

Meanwhile, our regular Open Doors work continued, including occasional courier trips into China with smaller amounts of Bibles. In early 1980, our coworker, Paul, hosted a meeting in Manila of the thirteen Open Doors researchers from bases around the world. Afterward they arranged to make a "standard" courier run into China from Hong Kong.

Paul's group had joined a larger tourist group, since individual tourism was not yet permitted in China. There were about sixty people altogether. All of the Open Doors staff passed through customs without any difficulty and were waiting on the bus for the others.

Suddenly one of the official tour guides came running up to the bus, saying, "Too many Bibles, too many Bibles!"

"What's going on?" the researchers said to each other. "We've already been through."

"Customs wants everybody back inside," the guide said. "Too many Bibles."

So they left their shoulder bags on the bus and went back into customs. As it turned out, two Christian Japanese tourists (unknown to our people) had brought Bibles and hymn books, but they had stuffed their bags so full that the books were poking out of the sides and caught the officials' attention. After this discovery, the customs agents thought, *Hmm, maybe there are others in this group with Bibles.* So they made all sixty people in the tour group open their bags, which had not yet been loaded onto the bus. They found nearly all of the Open Doors Bibles as well.

At first everyone was perturbed. The Japanese tourists were upset with the customs officials, the Open Doors people were upset that their cover had been blown by someone else's carelessness, and all the others who hadn't brought Bibles were upset that the Christians had disrupted their trip. It was indeed a strange situation. As all the Bibles and hymnals were confiscated and stacked on the customs counter, our group of researchers wondered, *Why would the Lord let this happen—especially after we had already made it through?*

It would not take long for the answer to become clear. Everyone was permitted to proceed with the tour; the Bibles and hymnals would be returned to them on the way out of the country. But since the discovery had caused a scene, it became a constant topic of conversation between the Christian and the non-Christian members of the tour group.

"Are you one of those who brought in Bibles?" was the typical question.

When our researchers would answer yes, the inevitable question was, "Why?"

"Well, because Christians in this country, from what I hear, are in desperate need of Bibles. So I tried to bring them some."

Frequently the conversations made it possible for our people to share their faith with the other tourists. Even the official Chinese guides became interested and talked at great length with some of the Christians about the meaning of faith.

Toward the end of the trip, the entire tour group sat down to an eighteen-course Chinese banquet. Normally at such a dinner, there would be no speaker or program, but on that occasion, the guide asked for volunteers to sing a song from their own country. Several stood and sang a native song, but then one of the Christians took his turn.

"You may not know it, but I'm a preacher," he said. "I would like to sing a song that everyone can learn. It's very easy—only one word: *Hallelujah.*"

As he started to sing, the other Christians joined in, then broke into four-part harmony until their singing filled the dining room. Next, another Christian sang "Seek Ye First the Kingdom of God." Then came "Amazing Grace" and several other hymns. At one point the tour guide broke in, not to stop the singing, but to ask if the group knew a particular melody. When he hummed the tune, they realized it was "Battle Hymn of the Republic," so they sang that, too.

Finally a Welshman from the Open Doors team offered up an old Welsh hymn, saying that it described the most important Person in his life. The words spoke powerfully of the blood of Christ and his death on the cross for the sins of the world. When he had finished, the whole room fell silent. For at least a minute, no one moved or spoke. It seemed that everyone present— Christian and non-Christian, the tour guides, even the kitchen staff who listened from the doorways—had been deeply touched by the events of the evening.

On the final day, one of the guides asked, "Could you give me one of those Chinese Bibles that you have? I'd like to read it." Our people had managed to bring in plenty of Scriptures in their shoulder bags, and they were more than happy to comply. Meanwhile, another believer had offered to give the same guide his English study Bible as well. When the time came to leave, he asked the guide if he still wanted it.

"Oh, yes, very much," the guide replied. "But don't give it to me now—I'm being watched. After we go around the corner, you can give it to me."

A few moments later the guide had a Bible in both Chinese and English. And all those on the Open Doors team realized that what they may have *thought* was a failed courier run had actually turned into a wonderful opportunity to share Christ with many who would never hear about him otherwise. I love that story because it shows so clearly how Christians can not only take the initiative and go into "enemy" territory, but they can *retain* that initiative even when things don't work out exactly as planned.

‹o›

Only a few months later, we were busy planning an extraordinary operation that would make Project Rainbow seem minuscule. When the Kwangs had first arrived in Hong Kong, they had told us of the need for thirty thousand Bibles. But thirty thousand was only the tip of the iceberg.

"That will satisfy our immediate needs," they had said, "but our overall need is for one million Bibles."

A *million*? That many Bibles was almost beyond comprehension. Especially considering that the Kwangs were one family ministering in just one part of China. They were asking only for enough Scriptures to handle the needs they knew of personally! When I heard of the colossal request, my immediate response was yes. I have to admit, I had no idea how many one million Bibles was; nor did I know how we'd be able to take in such an amount. I don't think the Chinese believers really knew what they were asking for, either. But like young couples who on their wedding day say "I will" and then realize later what they've gotten themselves into, we accepted the challenge and trusted God to show us the ways and means.

So after the success of Project Rainbow, we knew it was time to pray about supplying the one million. We dubbed the new operation Project Pearl because the Scriptures are like the "pearl of great price" Jesus referred to in the parable of the merchant (Matthew 13:45–46 NKJV). And like the merchant, the Chinese Christians were willing to risk everything for the "pearls" of God's Word.

The Kwangs had further indicated that the believers wanted the entire shipment at once. The safety of our delivery team was one of their chief concerns. They felt that one trip with a million Bibles would be much less risky than ten trips with one hundred thousand. And they had even provided an idea about how to get the "pearls" into the country. On the southern coast of China near the city of Swatow, there was a village in which a majority of the people were Christian. If the Bibles could be dropped on the beach close to that town, a virtual army of believers would be able to collect, store, and distribute them quickly.

The beach was their idea. But how to get the Bibles there? That's what we had to figure out. So the Open Doors Asia team and I spent many hours in prayer and conducted a lot of research. In the process, God brought two remarkable men into the picture. The first was James, a former officer in the U.S. Navy with a doctorate in management. He happened to be serving on Open Doors' board of directors and took a great deal of interest in the project.

James went to some of his friends who worked in a Washington, D.C., think tank and gave them an assignment: "If you had to move 232 tons of cargo into a foreign country surreptitiously, how would you do it?" He did not tell them the country or the nature of the cargo. His friends agreed to research the possibilities and provide him with an unofficial strategy.

Several months later they presented him with their conclusions. The cargo would be too heavy to transport by air, they said. The only way to do it was by water. So far so good. We had already been offered a beach by the believers, so a water delivery made sense.

The men at the think tank had devised an elaborate plan that involved a barge towing cargo barrels underwater. A pulley system would then draw the barrels from the water up to the beach. Although we decided their plan was too complicated, it was well thought out and gave us lots of ideas. For one thing, we realized that a tugboat pulling a barge was a common sight all over Asia. Perhaps there was a simpler way to use the tug/barge combination to make the delivery.

At that point God brought to us the second key person in Project Pearl, Bill. One of the original Jesus People from San Francisco, Bill had moved to the Philippines during the early 1970s and started the Jesus People movement there among university students. (The movement is still going strong in the Philippines under the name Solid Rock.) Once the group had become firmly established, Bill stepped down and began his own boating business on the Philippine island of Mindoro.

That was where Brother David and Paul Estabrooks, project coordinator for Pearl, first met him. They were very impressed with his personality and his credentials. Not only was he a committed Christian, but he was an experienced captain who knew the ways of the sea. At age fifty, he had no college degrees, but he possessed a brilliant analytical mind and a strong creative instinct. He was a true Renaissance man who would be the perfect captain for Project Pearl. We all prayed about it and before long the Captain, as we called him, came on board.

Working closely with James and the Asia project team, Bill plunged into the task of masterminding a workable plan for a water delivery. Carrying the million Bibles by barge posed no major problem; the main difficulty lay in getting the cargo from the barge to the shore. How could it be done simply and swiftly?

None of us could have fathomed the ingenious idea they came up with. The Captain designed a whole new barge with a special feature: the ability to partially submerge itself. It would be able to take on water and "sink" until the main cargo deck dropped below the surface. The cargo, which would be wrapped in water-tight plastic, would then float. Side doors on the barge would be electrically lowered, and the 232 one-ton parcels could be towed to shore with a few small powerboats.

Then there was the matter of the tugboat. We had determined that it needed to sleep twenty men, but no tug is built that way. Most sleep four or five. After much searching throughout East Asia, we found one in Singapore that was built but not outfitted, so we were able to have it altered to handle twenty people. The cost? A cool $480,000, which we discovered was actually a good price. We scraped together a $100,000 down payment from our various Open Doors bases, but the remainder had to be paid within thirty days. To our amazement and gratitude, the entire balance was covered by the generosity of just one church, Calvary Chapel in Costa Mesa, California. Pastor Chuck Smith personally organized the final $380,000 payment in the nick of time.

We decided to name the tugboat *Michael* and the barge *Gabriella,* after the only two angels mentioned by name in the Bible, Michael and Gabriel. There was a double significance to the names, however, because we had also given the Christian names Gabriella and Michael to Mama and Papa Kwang when they came out of China.

As construction began on the barge, the team whittled away at the endless details of planning and strategizing. Most of the planning took place in Manila and Hong Kong, but on many occasions we got together in my office in Holland to go over the arrangements. We spread maps and photos of the beach provided by the believers all over the floor. Again and again we studied every square foot of sand, every little tree, every possible approach to the beach. We discussed and prayed and modified plans as we went along.

After we solicited bids from publishers around the world, Thomas Nelson Publishers in the U.S. agreed to print the Bibles for $1.25 each—cheaper than Taiwan, Korea, anywhere. Of course, once we added in the huge overhead expenses—largely related to security—the total cost would be about $7 per Bible, delivered. We had to spend a lot of extra money to maintain secrecy and keep everything under our control. We could have rented the barge and tug for less, for instance, but typically renters are not allowed to use their own personnel. And we would not have been able to customize the boats to fit the special needs of this task.

I traveled and spoke in Europe and America to raise funds for the project, mentioning the goal of a million Bibles into China but not the way it would be done. Pat Robertson of the Christian Broadcasting Network generously allowed us to make a promotional video in his studio free of charge, including his own time. Pat and I discussed on the video the great needs of the Christians in China and our aim of providing one million Bibles. As part of our pitch, Pat said, "But, Andrew, why are they so expensive—seven dollars each?"

"Okay, Pat," I said, "here is a Chinese Bible. I want you to go to China and personally give it to a Chinese pastor. Then come back and tell me how much it would cost."

"Well, I'm sure it would cost me thousands of dollars," Pat replied.

"Tell you what," I said, "I'll do it for only seven dollars."

We all decided early on that utmost secrecy was essential if we were to succeed. Even more important, however, was to surrender every person, every task, every detail of Project Pearl to the Lord in prayer.

◄◦►

I made several trips into Hong Kong and China to prepare for Project Pearl. In Hong Kong I prayed and planned with the Kwangs and with our team, and in China I visited house churches and met secretly with some of the local leaders. On one visit with a colleague, Terry, we smuggled in a movie camera and a suitcase full of film, and filmed several house-church meetings and interviews with church leaders.

Again I was so impressed with the young people, brave souls who boldly proclaimed their faith under seemingly impossible conditions. One group of young Christians lived on the first floor of a house where government employees occupied the second floor. The only bathroom was on the first floor, so the officials would have to walk through the Christians' home to use the bathroom.

And yet the courageous young people were full-time Bible distributors and held covert church meetings in that apartment! They took me into the bedroom and showed me how they stashed Scriptures under their beds. I was amazed.

Knowing that in China's communist system those who didn't work went to prison, I asked them why they did not have to work a regular job.

"Because on the job we witness," they replied.

"Then why don't they put you into prison?"

"Because in prison we witness, too."

Seeing that kind of determination to spread the gospel regardless of the cost gave me even greater confidence that Project Pearl would be a success.

Many other fearless Christians in China were busy laying the groundwork for Pearl. Some helped to organize the storage and distribution network, others monitored police activity patterns in the area of Swatow, and still others planned and enlisted helpers for the beach landing. A Chinese team member, Joseph, went in and out of China through Hong Kong and stayed in contact with the believers.

As we continued our meeting and planning outside China, our chief strategist, James, wanted more specific information from the believers inside. He also wanted to be sure that they realized the immensity of the task and were willing to accept the risks. So Joseph went in and met with the five house-church leaders who were the key organizers of the project inside China. He sat down and said, "I have a list of questions that my colleagues have asked me to ask you."

"Go ahead," they said.

"First of all, do you know how much space one million Bibles take up?" He explained that they would fill about twenty rooms of that size from floor to ceiling, wall to wall.

"Joseph," they said, "we know how many it is. We have a plan. We have already prepared some storage places. You just bring them."

"Okay," he said. "Second question: Do you know what could happen to you if you were caught with even a portion of this many Bibles?"

"Joseph, all five of us have been in prison for the Lord over and over again. If you add up all the years, we've spent a total of seventy-two years in jail for Jesus. We are willing to die if it means that a million brothers and sisters can have a copy of God's Word."

Tears came to Joseph's eyes. He sat there quietly with them for a moment, then folded up his long list of questions and put it away.

When he returned to Hong Kong, he told the Asia team, "I just couldn't ask them any more questions."

Some of those house-church leaders were indeed persecuted after Pearl, but from the very beginning they had been prepared to die if necessary in order to see it accomplished. To them it was a matter of life and death.

After a year of intense planning, we locked in the date for the beach delivery: the night before Easter Sunday, April 19, 1981. There are too many instances for me to recount in which God miraculously worked out personnel and arrangements and finances. By the time April rolled around, we were absolutely certain Pearl would be a success.

Chapter Seven

◄o►

Twenty-one Teacups, Eighteen Bowls of Rice

I sat up in my bed in Holland, puzzled and perplexed. It was sometime in the middle of the night, Palm Sunday, 1981—one week before Project Pearl's scheduled beach delivery. I had just had a dream. I was riding in a truck, going down a long, steep hill in the Alps. As I put my foot on the brake to slow the vehicle, the brakes lost all pressure and the pedal went to the floor. I was careening down the hill, faster and faster, with no way to stop the truck. At the bottom I managed to avoid a huge crash by swerving onto a mound of gravel, which somehow brought the truck to a stop, leaving me sitting there with my heart pounding.

The dream disturbed me a great deal. What could it mean, if anything? I was too upset to go back to sleep, so I lay there in bed and replayed it in my head over and over, praying that God would reveal its meaning.

I had a strong feeling that the dream related to Project Pearl. The Captain and his crew of twenty men were preparing to set sail from Hong Kong in a couple of days. My team in Holland had been praying and fasting and keeping in constant phone contact with the project leaders. Pearl had been on my mind and in my prayers day and night for weeks, if not months.

By morning I was convinced that God was sending a warning —not to call off the project, but to wait. Something about the timing was not right. If we were to proceed, some kind of disaster would occur.

I phoned Johan and the management team and asked them to meet me at the office right away. There I went over the dream with them, and we discussed it and prayed about it at length. They agreed with me that it was significant enough to call a temporary halt to the project. Next, I called Sealy Yates, chairman of the Open Doors board of directors, who suggested that I meet with him and the board and Brother David in California. Finally I dialed Brother David in Hong Kong. He and the Captain and the crew were in the midst of loading the barge with Bibles.

"David," I told him, "I had a dream last night, and I believe it was the Lord telling us to postpone this project."

"What? You've got to be kidding!"

"I'm afraid I'm not kidding. I've talked and prayed about it with the team here and with Sealy, and we all feel we should halt everything for the time being. Bill and the crew should remain there with the ship and wait. We are not going to make any further decisions just yet. You come to the States, and we'll all get together and pray and fast and talk."

Brother David and the crew were crushed. If God had really wanted to postpone the mission, wouldn't he have given a sign to others as well? Perhaps, but not necessarily.

I knew how much hard work, training, prayer, and sacrifice the twenty crew members had undergone. They had been carefully selected from Open Doors bases around the world. Each man had been interviewed and asked to explain why he felt God was leading him to the assignment. I had also urged the leaders to be sure each man had the complete support of his wife because all crew members would need to spend several months away from their families.

Because Pearl was both clandestine and illegal, it could be a matter of life and death for those directly involved. Each team member was required to sign a letter absolving Open Doors from responsibility in case of imprisonment or death. To ensure the men's safety as well as the success of the delivery, we had insisted that each participant maintain total secrecy. They had agreed to tell no one except their wives about anything related to Pearl, and their wives had been given only the bare minimum of necessary information. Once the crew members had left their homes, they had known they would not be able to return until the operation was over. It was almost like being quarantined.

During that time they had been training and practicing dry runs at Captain Bill's cove on Mindoro Island in the Philippines. Only the Captain and James really knew the ways of the sea, and they more than had their hands full whipping the rest of the landlubber crew members into shape. I heard many funny stories about some of the men. One guy didn't know where the deck was, and when he heard the order "All hands on deck!" he ran up with the others, frantically looking for a place to lay his hands on and pray. Others couldn't figure out the difference between the port and starboard sides of the boat. Still others had to deal with regular bouts of seasickness. By the time they arrived in Hong Kong to load the Bibles, however, everyone was excited and ready for the expedition. Even more, we were all totally convinced that God would bring success to the mission.

But then came the dream and our decision to halt the project.

It was a huge disappointment for all of us. Believe me, I didn't want to stop it, but I just couldn't ignore the warning from God. After all, we had listened to his promptings when they urged us to move forward; shouldn't we also listen when he told us to hold back?

I met with the board of directors in California for the rest of Easter week. After many hours of prayer and of reexamining every detail of Pearl, we arrived at a difficult decision: not to proceed—not to scrub the mission, but simply to wait until we felt God telling us what to do next.

Meanwhile, the poor crew spent Easter Sunday anchored in Hong Kong harbor, having a Communion service and trying to celebrate Christ's resurrection in spite of their disappointment. After working and praying so hard, they had not accomplished what they came to do. They were sitting right there on the boat loaded with a million Bibles, all ready to go, but they weren't going. Even worse, they didn't know if they'd ever be going. It was a very downer day.

And if it was a bad day for our people, it was a devastating one for the believers in China. We had tens of people involved; they had *thousands.* Word of the postponement was quickly sent to the Chinese Christian leaders, but they were unable to contact all of their workers in time. Many who hadn't heard the news showed up at the beach anyway on the night before Easter, only to discover that we had stood them up. They, too, were very disappointed.

The waiting was the hardest part, for them and for all of us. We were struggling together to listen to the Lord's leading, overcome various differences in management style, and carefully examine our options for Pearl. The process took several months, and brought both good and bad consequences with it. Several crew members needed to get back to their families or had other commitments and had to be replaced. The most serious loss was James, our chief strategist, naval expert, and first mate to the

Captain. Second mate Paul stepped up and assumed James's duties, while other replacements had to be quickly trained.

Waiting was hard for the Captain, too, even though he supported me and the board in our decision. (As it turned out, he had also been given a dream much like mine on the very same night, but I didn't learn of it until years later.) Like the rest of the crew, he was primed to move ahead, but in addition, he bore the final human responsibility for safely getting *Michael* and *Gabriella* to Swatow and back. I know he felt a great deal of inner turmoil about the delay.

I can't point to an exact moment in which God led us to give the go-ahead for another try. After continued prayer and many long days going over every facet of the operation, we finally felt that the project could move forward. The initial timing had been my main concern. So the Pearl leadership team put their heads together to set a new date and time.

We were already into May, and June was the last month of good weather before the typhoon season, so it had to be sometime in June. The tide and darkness were the other two crucial factors. High tide would allow them to get as close to the shore as possible, and of course, the darkness would provide maximum camouflage. By studying the tidal charts, they determined that high tide came at 9:00 P.M. on June 18, so that became the new D-day.

First, the receiving and distribution network of Chinese believers needed to be alerted. Even more, they needed reassurance that the delivery would actually take place. The Asia team had stayed in touch with them during the entire waiting period by means of Chinese "runners" who went in and out of the country with detailed updates from both sides of the operation. Also, Mama Kwang would phone certain leaders and pass on coded information.

As the crew prepared to leave at last, she called the believers again. "By faith we are ready to move the patient if the hospital is ready to receive," she said in Chinese.

"We are ready to receive!" was their enthusiastic answer. "Just one thing we would ask of our friends," they continued. "If the patient dies after the injection, neither of us is to blame the other."

"In other words," the interpreter said, "they are saying we must all be prepared for any suffering that might take place for Jesus' sake. Both sides now lay down their lives before him."

David called his wife to say that everything was a go. She then phoned me in Holland, and I sent out an urgent communique to every Open Doors base around the world: *Chinese courier team in danger. Please pray for seventy-two hours.* Each base in turn notified its staff, supporters, and prayer chains, and in a short time thousands of people worldwide were praying earnestly for Project Pearl.

The tugboat *Michael* weighed anchor, and soon she and the crew were on their way, with the barge *Gabriella* and its precious cargo in tow. A radio message was then sent from the boat to the Hong Kong base, which Mama Kwang then delivered by phone to the Christian leaders in China: "We are going to have a dinner party. Expecting so many people that we have arranged twenty-one teacups and cooked eighteen bowls of rice." The numbers twenty-one and eighteen stood for the hour and the date of the mission—2100 hours on June 18.

The next day came the believers' reply: "Welcome to the party!"

For the most part, the three-day journey up the China coast was uneventful. The crew spent much of the time in prayer. As they approached the Swatow harbor on June 18, they were greeted by excellent weather, a calm sea . . . and Chinese patrol boats. A major naval base was nearby, but the crew had not expected to brush so closely with the navy itself. During the day a huge ship full of troops passed within five hundred feet of *Michael*. And in the distance gunboats patrolled the waters.

As the daylight turned to dusk, however, one of the gunboats left the other harbor traffic and headed straight for our expedition. The Captain quickly alerted the crew. Everyone prayed silently and tried to look nonchalant.

The forty-five-foot craft drew closer and closer until our crew could easily see the manned machine gun on the stern deck. Then it pulled within seventy-five feet of *Michael*.

"O, Lord, O, Lord," one of the crew said, gripping the wheel tightly to keep the tug on course.

Everyone held his breath. On the bridge, the Captain gazed straight ahead and muttered, "If you don't look at me, I won't look at you."

As it turned out, that is exactly what happened. Neither the gunner nor the captain of the patrol boat even turned his head in *Michael*'s direction. It was almost as if they didn't even see her. A few minutes later it was gone.

Our crew praised God for his protection. They were only an hour away from "Mike," their code name for the appointed beach. As darkness fell, they turned off their running lights and quietly maneuvered through several troop carrier ships anchored in their path. Then, with a continued sense of God's presence, they slowly headed toward the shore. The ocean conditions could not have been more perfect. Darkness had fully settled in, and the sea was virtually calm.

Finally "Mike" came into view. The beach looked completely deserted, with its bare three-hundred-yard stretch of sand flanked by a grove of trees, but the crew knew better. At exactly 9:00 P.M., David flashed a bright hand-held light three times toward the shore for one last confirmation. Even then, the Chinese Christian leaders could scrub the mission if necessary, and *Michael* and *Gabriella* would quickly steal away. He was answered right away with three matching flashes from the trees.

The Captain turned the tug so *Gabriella* would swing around as close to the shore as possible. He cut the engines and lowered the anchors. Then the men on the barge began the process of taking in water to submerge the deck loaded with the huge blocks of Bibles. Others lowered the three Zodiac rubber power-boats into the water. David and two other crew members hopped into one of the boats and made their way to shore, where the Chinese leaders were waiting. They embraced joyfully and, after pausing for a few moments of prayer, signaled for the transfer to begin.

Everyone leaped into action. Crew members on the barge pumped more water into one side so it would tilt the cargo into the sea; then they dropped the side doors that held it in place. All 232 blocks of Bibles had been roped together so they could be pulled to shore in a massive chain. As the side of the barge tipped below water level, the huge blocks were muscled into the sea and the three Zodiac boats began towing them toward the beach.

Meanwhile, the once-bare strand had undergone a dramatic transformation. Some two thousand Chinese believers had emerged from the shadows and descended upon the beach, wading neck-deep into the water and forming a brigade-style line all the way back to the trees. As the blocks reached them, they dragged them ashore, cut open the waterproof packaging with shears, and then passed the boxes one by one to the top of the line. Each one-ton block contained forty-eight boxes with ninety Bibles per box. (The box size was intentional so that two at a time could be easily carried using the traditional bamboo rod over the shoulders. Lasso ropes were also provided so people could carry two boxes on the back of a bicycle.)

At one point, several local people who happened to be fishing came onto the scene. Without flinching, the Chinese Christians simply asked them to join in and help, which they gladly did.

Once the boxes reached the tree line, they were piled onto

waiting bicycles, cars, and trucks, which immediately vanished into the night to prearranged locations. We had sent in about $75,000 ahead of time for the believers to rent vehicles and to facilitate the distribution of the Bibles.

Amazingly all 232 tons of Scriptures—11,136 boxes—were on the beach in less than two hours. That works out to nearly two tons a minute, using nothing but human strength, a few rubber boats—and the awesome power of God. The exhausted, exhilarated team left at eleven o'clock, remaining quiet until they reached international waters, then bursting into hoots and hollers of praise.

Back at the beach, however, the work had just begun. Many of the Bibles had already been whisked away, but the immediate task was to move all the remaining boxes into the trees and bushes where they wouldn't be noticed. By 1:00 A.M., everything was off the beach and spread around the cove. More vehicles arrived and continued to carry off as many boxes as possible. Everything seemed to be going smoothly. By 3:00 A.M., two-thirds of the million Bibles were safely on their way to Christians throughout the south of China who had agreed to store and distribute them.

Then something went wrong.

We were not able to piece together exactly what happened until months later. Apparently, after the local fishermen had helped the believers earlier in the evening, they had gone into nearby Swatow and told a few people about all the activity. They had seen a bunch of Russians dropping off cargo at the beach, they said. (The entire Pearl crew had let their beards grow, so they looked like Russians to the fishermen.)

Word must have gotten around because at 3:00 A.M. an army patrol showed up at the beach, surprising the hundreds of Christians still loading up the Bibles. The patrol quickly rounded up the people and seized what they thought were the remaining boxes. (Most of those arrested were released shortly thereafter.)

Lugging the Bibles out to the sand, the soldiers first tried to burn them, but were unsuccessful because books are difficult to burn without some kind of fuel. So out of frustration they reportedly threw the books into the water.

The believers later told us that the next morning the water looked like congee (rice porridge) because all the Bibles were floating in the water with the white pages up. Some other local fishermen came and scooped them out of the water, and for days afterward, Bibles could be seen drying on people's rooftops. Eventually they were sold back to the Christians.

Initially our contacts feared that they might have lost a third of the whole shipment as a result of the raid. I was disturbed to think that more than three hundred thousand Bibles may not have made it to the believers. Reports from some Western Christians who had visited the area further confused the situation. They had heard that an incredible event had taken place and, when they saw the Bibles on the rooftops, concluded that it had been a failure. Other Christian ministry people who either misunderstood or disagreed with our methods spread similar stories. Some rumors even reached me in Holland, and since I wasn't on the scene to verify facts, I became concerned.

"What's going on?" I asked David over the phone. "I just heard a report saying that the operation was a disaster. What's happening?"

"I don't know exactly," David answered honestly. "We're still waiting for updated reports from the believers. But I do know that people are circulating false information."

To set the record straight, Brother David decided to call his friend David Aikman, an editor with *Time* magazine. Aikman put David in touch with *Time*'s Hong Kong correspondent, and a full-page report on Project Pearl appeared in the October 19, 1981, issue, based on the most reliable information we had at that point. It was titled "Risky Rendezvous at Swatow" and even included one of our photos of the barge being loaded with Bibles.

I felt somewhat uneasy about the *Time* coverage because that kind of publicity is not my style, but in that case it seemed necessary. Although no names were given of those directly involved with Pearl, my full name was mentioned as president of Open Doors. It later appeared in a Chinese newspaper as well. That meant, of course, that it would be years before I'd be able to visit China again.

Those were minor consequences of the article. More controversial were the responses of some Western missions groups, who feared that the publicity would provoke the Chinese government to close its borders completely to Western Christians and ministry organizations. Some groups were in the middle of official negotiations with the Chinese government at that time. Others objected to the illegality of the act or accused us of flaunting our success before the Chinese and the rest of the world. That was never our intention. The only reason we allowed the *Time* article was that so much misinformation was being publicized, we felt we needed to set forth the truth.

Not until months and even years after the piece in *Time* did we get the full picture of what happened to all the Bibles. We learned several important things. First, when the patrol arrived on the scene, it seized only a part of the remaining Bibles, not all of them. The Chinese Christians quietly continued removing more boxes that were spread out under the trees.

In addition, many non-Christians had come to the beach after hearing of all the activity. They also found some of the boxes and, figuring they had value, took them home. Since they weren't known to be Christians, their homes were never searched by the authorities. When the coast was clear, the nonbelievers quietly went to the Christians and said, "Want to buy a Bible?" We sent in money and bought most of them back for ten cents each. We figured that was very cheap, safe storage.

It took about five years for us to track all the Bibles, but we were able to determine that 98 percent of the delivery had actually been accomplished in 1981. The other 2 percent we had sent in later that year by courier. We figured that no more than ten thousand copies—1 percent—had been destroyed by the patrol. In fact, while they fussed over the boxes left at the beach, they neglected to pursue the hundreds of people and vehicles in Swatow and neighboring towns that were loaded down with Bibles—allowing them to get away easily. The rest of the shipment made its way to house churches throughout China, some as far as three thousand miles away. Since then, Pearl Bibles have been spotted in every province of the country, even in some Three-Self churches.

In spite of the controversy over the *Time* publicity, an amazing thing happened only a year after the article appeared: China's official Three-Self church announced that it was printing one million Bibles of its own for distribution in China. When I heard that news, I just smiled. I knew in my heart, and am still convinced of it, that they never would have done such a thing had we not smuggled in the first million. There's no way I can prove it; I just believe it's true.

Indeed, that was one of Pearl's objectives—to pressure the government to print more Bibles inside the country. We would never be able to continue supplying such huge numbers of Scriptures, so we could only hope that Pearl would prompt some kind of favorable official response. Bible smuggling is an embarrassment to the government of any country. The necessity of smuggling shows that the government represses religion, which makes it look bad in the eyes of the world. So when it becomes public knowledge, as in this case, authorities usually feel compelled to do something in response, if only to appease outsiders. Of course, we continue our smuggling efforts until we have clear evidence that believers can obtain Scriptures freely.

◄o►

I've talked mostly about the aftermath of Project Pearl from the Open Doors side. But what about those who organized Pearl from within China? Our delivery may have taken only two hours, but the actual distribution took several years. In the early planning stages, the house-church leaders had told us they were willing to suffer and even die so their brothers and sisters could have copies of God's Word.

I am thankful that no one had to die, but many of them did suffer. I was deeply grieved to hear that shortly after the Pearl Bibles had been carried away from Swatow, the organizers were betrayed to the authorities by—amazingly—a trusted Christian. They were beaten, interrogated, and thrown into prison. Again I alerted our worldwide prayer network to intercede on their behalf, and we sent in couriers with money to support their families. Eventually they were all released.

The police aggressively sought out those who helped to distribute the Bibles as well. One such man was Pastor "John," a seventy-year-old house-church leader in Swatow. He later told News Network International reporter Ron McMillan his story of unimaginable suffering and of God's miraculous intervention. I rely on Ron's account of John's experiences in the story that follows.

Pastor John received a consignment of ten thousand Bibles the day after Pearl. "I praised God for hours afterwards," he said. "I just hugged the Bibles, thanking him for his kindness in allowing us to have so many at one time."

John's role was to store the one-hundred-plus boxes and then discreetly pass them on to other distributors and individuals in the area. But he soon realized that would not be possible for some time. A member of his house church stopped him on the street and advised him to be careful.

"Have you heard the news?" his Christian brother said. "The

whole town is buzzing about what happened last night. The civic authorities are furious, and they're determined to trace every Bible and jail every person who handles one."

John did not fear the police; he had been interrogated and imprisoned before. But he was concerned for his flock—the hundreds in his house churches. Because the scale of Pearl was so large and the Pearl Bibles identifiable, the believers could be imprisoned as well. After praying about his dilemma and consulting with a local farmer friend, he decided to wrap and bury the load of Bibles under his friend's barn. Once the uproar died down, he'd dig them up and give them out to the Christians.

Several months later the authorities still had not eased up in their search. When Pastor John was finally brought into the police station for questioning, he was surprised to see that his four interrogators were not local men but special investigators flown in from Beijing. In other words, the search for the Pearl ringleaders was being conducted at the national level.

The officials had pretty much decided ahead of time that John was one of Pearl's primary organizers. He was a prominent leader of the house churches—the group the Bibles were destined for, and he lived in Swatow—the location of the delivery. Since their minds were already made up, John did not try to convince them otherwise. As the interrogators pressured him for names of others involved in Pearl, he remained silent.

"I had gone through all this before during the Cultural Revolution," he recalled, "so I knew how to handle this kind of interrogation: Just shut your eyes and pray."

His reaction only infuriated the investigators all the more. In desperation, they resorted to an especially cruel means of torture. Taking John into the prison courtyard, they tied his hands behind his back and made him stand on a wooden box about four feet high and less than a foot wide. Then they placed a noose around his neck and attached the rope to a wooden beam above his head.

"We have given up on you," the officials said. "The moment you sway violently or your legs collapse with fatigue, you will hang yourself. It is a just penalty for your stubbornness." Then they left.

Two policemen were assigned to watch Pastor John's last moments. John looked down on them from his shaky perch. They hardly glanced at him, choosing instead to play a few gambling games.

"I felt like Christ on the cross," he recalled. "He must have felt the same way when he looked down and saw the soldiers casting lots for his clothes."

John felt a surge of power in his body and began to tell his guards about Jesus—his life, his death for our sins, and his resurrection. Because of what Jesus had done, John said, he was not afraid of death.

"Old man," one of the guards chortled, "when I reach seventy and look as unhealthy as you, I won't be afraid of death, either."

Soon the hours became days. John's body cried out for sleep, but he knew what would happen if he drifted off. His legs developed ferocious cramps, and in shaking them he nearly lynched himself. As the blood collected in his legs, they swelled to twice their normal size until numbness set in.

His only relief was the rain. He stuck out his thickened tongue to gain a few drops of moisture. It also seemed to wash his filthy body.

Five days passed. Then six. Then seven. Still John had not toppled over and died. Word was getting around the prison. No man could survive that long. He had been standing all that time, with no food, almost no water, and especially no rest.

Ten days passed. Eleven. Twelve. John was delirious, beyond feeling. On the thirteenth day, the sky blackened and a huge thunderstorm swept in. As he stood there pelted by the rain, his resistance gave out. A sudden flash of lightning and a simultaneous clap of thunder caused him to pitch forward. The noose tightened.

The next thing he knew, John heard himself coughing. He was no longer standing but lying on the floor. His legs had been propped up on a chair, and he could feel the blood flowing back into his upper body. The pain was excruciating. Someone was giving him water, then shaking him, trying to revive him. Barely able to open his eyes, he realized it was the two policemen.

"Please," they shouted, "don't die—please!" John managed to clear his brain for a moment.

"Why?" was all he could say.

"Because we want to know your Savior, Jesus," they replied, trembling.

"But why?" he asked again.

"Because he saved you!" they exclaimed. "A bolt of lightning cut the rope above your head just as you fell. Don't tell us that's a coincidence!"

They believed. And as the story spread, many others inside and outside the prison were profoundly affected by John's faith. Not knowing what else to do, the prison officials later released him.

It was 1985 before John was able to dig up the Project Pearl Bibles—four years after they had been delivered. He distributed them without any difficulty. In fact, the need for Scriptures had increased significantly during those years, and the "fresh" supply eased the shortage.

Did Pastor John and the other Chinese believers have any regrets about Project Pearl? We all wanted to know because even though we had financed and carried out a major portion of the task, it had been *their* initiative, their urgent request to us from the beginning. Was it worth all the suffering it had brought them?

John's amazing answer was echoed by many others.

"I was surprised twice over the whole affair," he said. "First, that Christians—Chinese and Western—actually had the courage and the vision to mount something this big. And second, that it was never repeated."

Step Six

─◄○►─

Maximize your opportunities by being present.

On my very first trip to Poland forty years ago, the Cold War was quite young, and no one really knew what conditions were like. I wasn't sure what evidence of life I'd find among the persecuted believers. I kept wondering how I could help them in their plight or what I might say that would give them hope and encouragement.

Much to my surprise, I found myself standing before a crowded church—alive, vibrant, and full of young people. As the pastor introduced me, he said, "Andrew, your being here means more than ten of the best sermons."

Well, that was okay with me, since I'm not much of a preacher anyway. But as I thought about the pastor's words, I realized he had said something extremely significant. Not that preaching was unimportant, but that my *presence* was much more important. I simply needed to be there!

When I speak of presence, I mean that we consciously steer our lives into danger areas. We go there in person. Not to start a church or heal the sick or sponsor a big campaign, but simply to bring the presence of Christ into that situation. Jesus said, "Blessed are the peacemakers." Peacemakers can make peace only where there is war. The people around us may not yet know that we are Christians, but at this stage all they need to see is our presence. Think of it: If Jesus lives in me, and I go to a trouble spot in the world, then Jesus is there, too. And once we are there, we see opportunities we would never hear about by staying behind because the opportunities didn't exist then. They come into being only the moment we get there.

Back in the 1950s an American by the name of Christy Wilson went to live in Afghanistan, a Muslim country with no missionaries and almost no Christians. Though he was not allowed to proselytize, he still believed he could have an impact for Christ in that country just by being there and watching for opportunities. Before long he and a few other foreign Christians who happened to work in the country formed a small house church. Then one of the elders who was a brilliant agriculturalist discovered that much of the fish in the country's rivers was of an inferior quality and undesirable to many. With Christy's help, the man imported rainbow trout eggs from the U.S., set up his own hatchery, and then proceeded to stock Afghanistan's lakes and rivers with the trout—much to the delight of the king and the people.

On another occasion, the king came to him for assistance in introducing a certain kind of duck into the country. The ducks would reduce the slug population and make it profitable for farmers to raise silkworms rather than opium. So Christy contacted some friends in Long Island, New York, who sent him duck eggs, and before long Afghanistan had its ducks. As a result, he gave a significant boost to the poor country's economy as well as its ecology, and was praised by the leaders of the country. Because of his contributions, it is no small wonder that then President Eisenhower helped him obtain permission to build the first evangelical church ever erected in Afghanistan. (The timing was perfect; Eisenhower had just allowed the Muslims to build the first mosque in Washington, D.C.) All of that happened simply because Christy went there and looked for ways to serve the people.

Looking back, I think I have operated in a similar way, though I didn't recognize it as such until more recently. Whenever I have traveled to trouble spots around the world, I didn't go in with a carefully worked-out strategy. All I knew was that I had to be there. I firmly believed that once I arrived, God would show me what to do next. And inevitably I would meet new friends, make important new contacts, witness a significant event, or find myself in a unique situation to share Christ. It has happened to me again and again—too many times to count.

I am not suggesting that we barge into an area blindfolded and avoid the homework we need to do to understand a country and its people. Planning, as I mentioned in step two, is extremely important. But the *agenda* must be God's agenda and not our own. By being there and allowing him to direct us to the right people and situations, we may actually be able to accomplish more for his kingdom.

A few years ago, I visited Beirut with my youngest son. As we were browsing in the Bible society bookshop, the general secretary of the Baptist Union of Lebanon walked in. I already knew him from my many previous visits. He greeted us warmly and then said something to my son that I will never forget.

"When everybody else runs away, your father comes to us," he said. "His being here is our greatest encouragement."

Our presence in a certain place has great value in the sight of God. This is true not only for me, but for every Christian—

famous or not, great preacher or not. Why? Because through us, the presence of Jesus *will* bring about change in whatever situation we find ourselves. It cannot be otherwise. We can all make a difference just as the Chinese house-church leaders did when they brought Christ's presence with them into prison and converted the guards and other inmates.

If we aren't having an effect on others, then we must honestly ask ourselves, Does Jesus really live in me? I am talking now about the very essence of the gospel: "Christ in you, the hope of glory" (Colossians 1:27). Without his presence, there is no hope for the world. And without our presence, there is little hope for the suffering people in closed countries—Christian or non-Christian.

Remember the two Dutch women in chapter three who traveled to Cuba without a plan and waited until God led them to the local minister badly in need of encouragement? They knew the importance of presence. For the same reason, I have preached in secret church meetings in the forests of Russia, and conducted services in the African jungle during which soldiers protected us with machine guns. I have shared Christ in communist training camps in Angola, at Middle Eastern terrorist bases, and among guerrillas in El Salvador. In the next chapter I tell about an Open Doors staff worker who changed an entire Mexican village by going there and bringing the presence of Christ into an oppressive situation. None of these opportunities would have arisen had we not personally been there.

How I wish that our Bible colleges and seminaries and missionary schools would teach the importance of presence evangelism! Then we would be able to send out ten times as many missionaries, and we wouldn't waste so much time fretting about our grandiose plans for churches, schools, hospitals, and radio stations. They are important, too, but they don't come until after we've been there. Get in first. Then see how God works.

PRAYER

*Lord, show me how I can bring your presence
to the places it is needed most,
simply by being there myself.
Amen.*

Chapter Eight

◄○►

Children of the Revolution

*M*any years had passed since I last visited Latin America, and it had undergone a great deal of upheaval in that time. During the late 1970s and early 1980s, the Marxist revolution that began in Cuba was spreading to other countries—and for good reason. The utter poverty, corrupt dictatorships, and the lack of law and order had created huge gaps between rich and poor, privileged and oppressed, left and right.

Backed by the Soviet Union, Fidel Castro and other revolutionaries provided—or more often imposed—what many thought was a viable alternative. Unfortunately the violence and the repression of the leftist leaders proved to be indistinguishable from those of the right-wing regimes.

As I followed the news reports and listened to stories from

friends of Open Doors in Latin America, I knew it was time for me to go back. I wanted to see for myself what was happening there. And most of all, I wanted to find out how the church was responding. How had things changed since my visit in the 1960s? Were believers still suffering for the cause of Christ? What kind of alternative were they setting forth?

So during the early 1980s, I visited most of the countries in Central and South America. I saw the social and political unrest, the governments left and right, stable and unstable, the ubiquitous military or paramilitary presence, the triple-digit inflation, and overwhelming poverty. I talked to left-wing guerrillas and right-wing extremists. I also met with Christians wherever I went, listening to their stories and offering encouragement.

In Brazil, for instance, I found a flourishing evangelical church estimated at the time to be twenty million strong (and closer to thirty million today). Many of them are Pentecostals, the fastest-growing body of Christians in all of Latin America. We want to encourage them to remember the suffering church on their own continent and around the world.

Brazil was more of an exception than the rule, however. In a majority of the countries I visited, some believers had experienced mild forms of persecution, while others had faced torture and prison—at the hands of both left and right.

Churches throughout Latin America responded in different ways to the revolutionary threat. Some dispersed or were closed by whoever was in power. Some, refusing to endorse either the right or the left, were persecuted for their lack of support.

Others felt compelled to take sides, and certain pastors and priests publicly identified with either left or right. One of the best known of those priests was Catholic Archbishop Oscar Romero, who was assassinated in 1980 for his leftist associations. I visited the site in El Salvador where thousands of mourners who had gathered for his funeral were ambushed by rightist machine-gun fire. Hundreds had died and hundreds more were injured.

While speaking at a seminary in Jamaica, I encountered a number of theologians who advocated the tenets of liberation theology—essentially the belief that our primary calling as Christians is to secure (with guns, if necessary) the liberation of the poor and oppressed. One professor, who called himself an evangelical, said that he liked what I had to say, and that he agreed with 90 percent of my theology. I wasn't so sure about that, so I challenged him.

"If I were to preach my message publicly here, would you kill me?"

Without flinching he said, "Yes, I would kill you."

"Well, thank you," I said, suddenly wanting to change the subject. "I'll have another cup of coffee now."

At least in Jamaica the seminaries let me speak. The seminaries in Costa Rica wouldn't allow us there at all. They were afraid of our simple message, which was not political but certainly radical: Anyone who enters into a relationship with Jesus will be transformed into his instrument for changing the world.

In Puerto Rico, I spoke to an unusual group of believers who went by the name of Catacombas. The leader, Pedro, had come up with the name after reading a book about the early Christians who, to escape persecution by the authorities, met for worship in the catacombs of Rome.

That particular group had cleared out a meeting place in the forest outside San Juan, and they sang to the Lord at the top of their lungs, accompanied by maracas, tambourines, and guitars. They also kept on hand a map of the subterranean drain system of the city, in case they would be forced underground like the ancient Christians.

"We have already seen what has happened in Cuba," he said. "Now Nicaragua has had its revolution, and El Salvador is in the middle of its own. We can see all these troubles creeping toward Puerto Rico. That's why we must prepare. We know that persecution can come from the left or the right, and we are willing to pay any price to keep our liberty as Christians."

I noticed large numbers of young people wherever I went. They comprised nearly half the population of Latin America, and always seemed to be the target of ideological campaigns from both right and left. One of Cuba's propagation methods paralleled that of the Soviets in Africa: They would recruit young people fresh out of high school, promise them a free education, and then keep them on the Isle of Pines (off the Cuban coast) for anywhere from four to seven years of Marxist indoctrination. After their training, they were sent back to their home countries as communist revolutionaries. I met many grief-stricken parents whose children were stuck in Cuba or even Russia, unable to return for years, if at all.

Another method was to sponsor a literacy drive. Schools and churches would be closed for a period of months while high-school-age kids taught those in the outlying areas how to read and write. When the campaign was over, communist propaganda was given to everyone, and very few of the young teachers would return to church.

When we came to Managua, Nicaragua, we learned the government was about to start a literacy campaign, which is a prerequisite for establishing communist rule. They intended to close the churches for three to six months, apparently because they were afraid that Scriptures and Christian literature would be distributed during the drive. Knowing the devastating effect closing the churches would have, I managed to contact the leader of that campaign, a Mexican intellectual, and arranged to have a meal with him.

We had a deep, serious talk. I don't know what I said, but I remember that the Lord guided me very strongly. In the course of that conversation, something happened and the leader agreed to change his plans. The literacy campaign went forward, but the churches stayed open. It was a great victory for the church and a hopeful sign for Nicaragua's youth.

On a follow-up visit to Cuba, I noticed a saying from revolutionary Ché Guevara chiseled into a hospital wall: "If this Revolution is not aimed at changing people, then I am not interested."

My first reaction was that almost sounded like a quotation from the New Testament. But after studying his writings further, I realized that Guevara had something different in mind: "Hatred is a factor in the struggle, unbending hatred of the enemy, which takes the individual beyond his natural limitations and transforms him into an effective, violent, selective and cold mechanism of death. That's how our soldiers must be. A people without hatred cannot win against our brutal enemy."

His words made me wonder when we would dare to declare publicly that no one can be used by God and bring peace anywhere in the world unless he has peace in his heart. We cannot be the solution if we are still part of the problem.

Finding realistic solutions to the problems facing Latin America seemed so utterly impossible to me at times. The greatest hope, I felt, was in conveying our message to the young people. And what was the message? That the love, the compassion, and the mercy of Jesus Christ embrace both right and left, and that only through him will there be lasting peace. When people allow Jesus to completely change them, they become part of the biggest revolution on the face of the earth. By recruiting young people and motivating them for Jesus, they can in turn win millions more from all over Latin America.

In 1984 we came up with Project Crossfire, an immense effort to provide New Testaments, Christian literature, and support to a Christian youth movement working throughout Latin America. Their goal? To evangelize other young people, and to give direction, purpose, and hope to new believers.

◄o►

Whenever I pick up a copy of *National Geographic,* I feel a special kind of challenge. Many times I have read of remote places in the world or primitive people never before visited by modern people. I wonder, Why do the journalists get there first? Why not representatives of Christ? We should have the same determination, the same fearlessness, and the same refusal to accept no as an answer that reporters and explorers and adventurers have. They manage to get in, so why do we say it is impossible or too dangerous for Christians?

I am happy to say that most of the Open Doors field staff have that pioneering attitude. They are fearless. They will go anywhere. Today, Richard Luna is our Latin American frontiersman. He pulls on his backpack and, with a small team of young people, disappears into the jungle for a week and visits the believers. He has gone to Peruvian villages inhabited only by wives and children—all the men have been kidnapped or killed. In Peru's guerrilla war, between twenty thousand and thirty thousand people have died, including seven hundred evangelical leaders.

One of these leaders, known as "Grandpa Sauñe," was brutally murdered by Shining Path guerrillas during Christmas of 1989 for the "crime" of preaching to the young people and encouraging them to join God's revolution of love rather than an atheistic one filled with hate and death. That same day forty-two of his relatives were also massacred. Three years later, his grandson, Romulo, was slain after visiting the community where his grandfather was killed. Romulo, the recipient of World Evangelical Fellowship's first religious liberty award, had served as the head translator for the Bible in his native Quechua of Ayacucho language.

I met Romulo's wife, Donna, and their four children at one of our prayer conferences. They remain in Peru, working closely with Open Doors to continue the work Romulo started.

It is because of Romulo and Donna and many other suffering believers in Latin America that we are there to help. We have distributed about thirty thousand Bibles and New Testaments in the last few years to strengthen those Christians in the jungle and the mountainous highlands. And we are now sending Agape Teams—mountain brigades of Open Doors staff and local volunteers—to bring the love of God to those who are struggling in remote areas. I believe these teams give us a glimpse into the future of how the Latin American church will reach its native peoples. But there is still plenty of risk involved. If we hear one day that Richard isn't coming back, we shouldn't be surprised.

I didn't know Richard when I visited Central America in the early 1980s. But in Mexico City I did meet a brave young woman, "Anna," who had the drive, the persistence, and the ability of a reporter. In fact, she *was* a reporter specializing in Latin American issues and religious freedom. She was also a dedicated Christian who cared deeply about the suffering church.

I told Anna of my desire to visit El Salvador, which at the time was in the midst of a civil war. I didn't simply want to get into the country, however; I wanted to talk directly with the leftist guerrillas, or rebels, who were trying to overthrow the government and its right-wing death squads. I also wanted to bring in a TV crew and make a film. Well, with all of the journalists and other contacts she knew, Anna was able to arrange the trip without a problem. And because she is fluent in Spanish, she acted as our field producer and interpreter.

Together our team of six roamed around the country for about ten days in a small red van. The TV crew had fastened a borrowed white towel to a broomstick and poked it out the side window at all times to indicate our political neutrality. But between the many checkpoints and the terrible dirt roads, driving was slow.

I will never forget the things I saw and the people I met in El Salvador. As we entered one bombed-out town, we met a group of guerrillas. With them was a girl carrying a bag of tomatoes. Her name was Maria, and she was only fifteen years old—the same age at that time as my daughter back in Holland.

"Why are you with this group of guerrillas?" I asked her.

She looked down. "I am looking for my father and my three-year-old sister." Apparently they had disappeared one night during a clash between the military and the locally based rebels, and Maria hadn't seen them since.

As I stood there under a big tree talking to her, I tried to imagine how I would feel if this were my daughter, wandering through the jungle in the company of heavily armed guerrillas, picking her way through bombed-out towns, searching not only for her father and little sister, but for meaning in life.

I met other young people with equally disturbing stories. Eleven-year-old Domingo was forced to flee his home, along with his mother, grandmother, and four brothers and sisters when his town came under siege. They walked for fifteen long days through mountains and valleys with nothing to eat until they reached a relatively safe camp for displaced people. There, Domingo had nothing to do but dream about the future, when (he hoped) things would be better and he could become a farmer. And like Maria, he, too, wondered where his father was.

Then there was fifteen-year-old Pedro, whom we met in another camp. "There was an attack in our village at about ten o'clock in the morning," he recalled. "As the people began running in all directions, the soldiers shot everyone, even the children and the old people. Helicopters were bombing the houses. My mother and I ran for the river to get away, and so did many others. But as we crossed the river, the soldiers came up and began shooting into the water. Many of the people were killed or shot so they then drowned. I will never forget the terrible moment when I saw my mother die in that river."

Through the ministry of an American Catholic priest, Pedro had become a Christian while staying in the camp. "I still don't know how I got away from the soldiers," he continued, "but I thank God I made it to this place. I am learning how to be a tailor. And I'm also learning about Jesus Christ. I now know that he is the answer that my country needs—that we all need."

When we arrived at another village, we had expected to see more guerrillas. But as it turned out, for that day at least, the government troops were in control. In the civil war, power and control shifted back and forth from town to town. I watched the young soldiers, many of them teenagers—heavily armed, motivated and dedicated, looking for their enemies.

I interviewed one boy on camera who carried an automatic rifle nearly as big as he was. I told him that when I was twenty-one, I had become a Christian and began to follow Jesus Christ. He said he was not familiar with Jesus or the Bible.

"Jesus also wants to make us soldiers in his army," I said to him. "Because we have to fight against sin in the world, and sin is also injustice. Jesus came to take the sin away, out of our hearts and out of the world. You know, the Bible would be a much better weapon to win the world than, uh, what you are carrying. Because it changes people, and when many people have changed, then the world will change."

He just smiled at me shyly, probably because he was being filmed.

One of my most memorable encounters was with Alberto, the commander of a group of rebels who had completely overtaken a certain town. A good-looking man with a striking presence, he wore a black beret, khaki shirt, blue jeans tucked into military boots, and a pistol at his thigh. Two bodyguards followed him everywhere, carrying large 50-caliber machine guns and wearing bandoleers across their chests.

I also noticed that Alberto was wearing two watches. "If one stops, I will still always know the time," he said. Obviously he was a well-trained and well-disciplined person.

First he told us about his background and his "lost youth," and how he had found new hope in Marxist teachings. After training in Cuba and even meeting Fidel Castro, he returned to his country with a real sense of purpose because, he said, the revolution would bring fairness to life in El Salvador. I was impressed by this intelligent young man, and I thought his revolutionary zeal would make for an interesting film segment.

"Alberto," I said, "I would like to interview you on camera, but under one important condition: You must tell me the truth. I am going to ask you a question, and I want you to look me in the eye and tell me man to man the absolute truth. Will you agree to that?"

He paused for a minute and looked around. "Yes, I will tell you the truth," he said. Something in me believed he would.

The crew started the camera equipment. Then I turned to Alberto and asked my first question.

"Is this your revolution or is it imported?"

I don't think he was prepared for such a direct question. The way he answered me was of critical importance, and he knew it. An awkward silence followed. He glanced around, perhaps to see how many others were within hearing range. I kept gazing into his face, and the cameras continued rolling. The man who only a moment ago had exuded such strength and confidence seemed quite vulnerable.

Finally he turned and looked me straight in the eye, just as he'd promised, and gave me his answer.

"It's imported."

What a huge admission, especially for someone so high in the guerrilla ranks. For some reason, the minute he was confronted with that kind of a reality check, he couldn't lie. With those two words he had revealed what the revolution was really about. It was manufactured, and it was being imposed on the people.

I have always preached and practiced that we must go to the people who need Jesus Christ before they turn to evil ideologies and then come back to us in violence or judgment. Yes, it means taking risks to cross boundaries, but that is inherent in the Great Commission. That is why one moment I would be talking with government troops, and another moment with guerrillas like Alberto—all in the same country, the same conflict.

But there can be no real winners there because the bombs and bullets do not represent the real war. That war is spiritual, a war over what people believe, what they say, what they do, and what they are willing to die for. That decides the outcome of a war. And the only way to win a spiritual war is with the sword of the Spirit, the Word of God, and with the word himself, Jesus Christ, the Prince of Peace.

◄o►

As part of her reporting duties, Anna spent a lot of time in Mexico working with churches and Christian communities undergoing persecution. Officially there was religious freedom, but at the local level some evangelical churches and groups—mostly in rural areas—were targeted for harassment and even violence.

That is still true today. In the Mexican state of Chiapas, for instance, more than thirty thousand believers have been kicked off their land because of their evangelical faith in Christ. Authorities in the town of San Juan Chamula refuse to grant permission for the believers to build their own church.

Anna had heard about one particular rural village in the state of Puebla. The evangelical church there was facing tremendous oppression at the hands of local officials and the Catholic parish with which they were closely allied. The Catholic church building was in a serious state of disrepair, and its leaders had demanded that the evangelicals help them rebuild the structure. The evangelicals had politely responded that they did not have the time and resources to put into a church they didn't worship in.

Because they had refused to bow to the town's unofficial power structure, the evangelicals had been accused of being reactionaries and troublemakers. They were subjected to threats, intimidation, and outright acts of violence. Their own church building had been torn down and rebuilt three times in just two years. The homes of Christians were being raided and even burned down. Their crops were being destroyed and their animals stolen. They were under constant harassment and siege.

Anna sent a messenger to the town with a letter for the evangelical leaders. She was concerned about them, she wrote, and she would like to interview them. Would they be willing to tell their story, how they have survived, what their faith means to them, and why they have chosen to stay in spite of all the stress and persecution?

Several days later the messenger returned with a letter from the evangelical leadership. "Yes, we will be at the church with the entire congregation and the whole leadership," it said. "We will meet with you at noon on Sunday."

Then the messenger produced another letter. It was from the mayor and his deputies in the town. "If you take one step into our village," it read, "we will kill you."

Nervous but undeterred, Anna organized a group of eight bodyguards, most of whom were indigenous Christians, to accompany her to the remote village. From the nearest city it was about a two-hour drive through the jungle over narrow mountain roads.

The closer their pickup got to the village, the more obstacles they encountered. At one point they saw five men laying out logs in the road.

"Oh, I recognize those guys," one of the bodyguards said. "They're known killers."

The driver stopped the pickup, and they watched in silence as the men finished their roadblock.

Finally Anna whispered, "Well, do you think you guys can move those logs?"

"Okay, we'll try." As they jumped out, the five men ran into the bush. So they heaved the logs aside, got back in the pickup, and kept going.

About a mile farther, a large platform truck coming from the direction of the town had stopped in the middle of the road, with the clear intent of blocking Anna's way. An older man sat behind the wheel, saying nothing; one of the bodyguards identified him as the brother-in-law of the mayor. On one side of his truck the mountain rose straight up, and on the other, it dropped off into a deep precipice. There was just possibly enough space between the truck and the edge of the cliff for them to get around.

Anna and her friends sat there for a few minutes, nose to nose with the other truck, trying to figure out what to do. She looked at the guys and said, "Can you drive around the truck? Is there enough space?"

"We don't know for sure, but we could try it."

Their main fear was that as soon as they started to go around, the big truck, which was still running, would nudge them off the side. So they came up with an unusual strategy: They would stare the truck driver straight in the eyes as they passed and try to unnerve him so that he would allow them through.

After sending up a quick prayer, they edged forward. Slowly, gingerly, they squeezed their pickup, slipping and sliding, around the side of the truck. All on board had turned and fixed their eyes right on the truck driver's face.

The strategy worked. Their penetrating stare caught the older man off guard, and he seemed to freeze in his seat. A moment later they were on their way again.

When they reached the village, they saw a sign posted prominently at the entrance that said in Spanish: WARNING: THIS IS A CATHOLIC VILLAGE. PROTESTANTS ARE NOT ALLOWED TO ENTER. THANK YOU VERY MUCH.

Talk about intimidation. They stopped again and discussed whether to continue. Anna refused to give up. She got out of the pickup and looked at the others.

"Well," she said, "I am going. You can come with me if you want, but you don't have to. This is what we in Open Doors are all about—to go where others won't go. I'm not going to ask you to risk your life because you may not have the same call I do. I am going to trust God to protect me as I go into this village."

They were all quiet for a moment. Then the bodyguards stepped forward and said, "We're going too." They all got back into the pickup and slowly proceeded into the village.

To their amazement, the streets were completely deserted. All the townspeople had retreated into their houses, and an eerie silence hung in the air. They could see faces staring at them through the doors and windows. That just doesn't happen at midday on Sunday in a Latin American village. It seemed like a showdown in one of those American Western movies.

Suddenly about ten men appeared from a side road and ran toward the pickup. Anna and the others prepared for an assault, but the men turned out to be Christian brethren who had been waiting for them. They jumped onto the sides of the pickup and held on, shielding the team from the view, and possibly the bullets, of the mayor's men.

"Drive as fast as you can," they said and directed them to the church. "Don't worry about us—we can hang on. You just drive fast."

They made it safely to the evangelical church compound, or what was left of it. All the Christians, about three hundred altogether, were standing in a circle around the perimeter of the property. The church had been destroyed, and there was rubble all around. They opened up a space in the circle for the truck to drive through and then closed in behind it. By then hostile villagers had also arrived and were trying to disrupt the meeting.

Anna jumped out and asked, "Where are the leaders?"

They stepped forward and immediately she began interviewing them, one by one, and taking pictures of the demolished church building. All the time the villagers were shouting, pushing, and shoving in an attempt to break the circle and arrest her, and the Christians were holding them off. It was an unbelievable scene.

Anna was concerned that at any moment the situation could get out of hand. She didn't see the mayor or any of his henchmen and wondered where he was. The whole time she was talking to the people, she had her eye on the jungle, looking for an escape route. *It will take me all day,* she thought, *but I know I can get back on foot if I bolt for the jungle.*

The interviews took about thirty minutes because many of the believers spoke only the indigenous language and needed interpreters. Fearing for her life, Anna had hoped to leave immediately after the interviews, but the women of the church had prepared lunch and they wanted their visitors to join them. So reluctantly they went in and sat down, planning to eat very fast so they could get out of there and possibly defuse the extremely tense atmosphere.

Before eating, the Christians asked their guests to pray. One of the men who had accompanied Anna was a pastor, so he offered a prayer to God for the food and for the dedicated brothers and sisters. As he was praying, Anna looked around and noticed that tears were streaming down many of the believers' faces, especially that of a young woman with a newborn baby in her arms. No one had ever shown any interest in their problems and their suffering and in all the stress and tension. No one had cared that their women were raped and their men were beaten and their belongings were repeatedly stolen. No one seemed concerned that they were rebuilding their church and their lives from scratch over and over again.

They all had a wonderful time together. The believers in that village didn't want anything material from Anna. All they wanted was spiritual communion and companionship. They needed to know they weren't alone in their struggle. To me that is what Open Doors is all about—going into the world and simply being there as the hands and feet of the Lord. Going to our hurting brothers and sisters and saying, "We are the Lord's presence with you. We share in your pain and we care that you are suffering."

After lunch Anna and her companions jumped back in the pickup and raced out of the town the same way they came. Shortly afterward the mayor and his deputies did come out, carrying rifles, but by then it was too late—the unwelcome visitors were gone.

There is an interesting footnote to this whole story.

A year later Anna was back in Mexico City, having lunch with the pastor who had actually gotten her into that village.

"Guess what?" he said. "Do you remember the village that we went to in Puebla where they threatened to kill us if we went in?"

"How could I forget?" Anna said.

"I thought you'd be interested to know this," he said. "After we left, the mayor and his cronies were deeply moved that someone from the outside would come to our country, to that tiny village, and listen to the concerns and struggles of that congregation. They were so impressed, in fact, that the mayor and several of his associates truly converted to Christ and then helped the believers rebuild their church. It has now been rebuilt, and the mayor himself worships there. And in that village there is now peace."

It was all because somebody came and said, "I care about you. I don't like to see you suffering, and I represent many other Christians who don't like it, either. We stand with you as fellow believers."

Reflecting on her experiences in Puebla and throughout Central America, Anna said, "Anyone could have done what I did. Anyone who is willing to do what God has called her to do and trust God to protect her.

"A lot of people said I had great courage during my years in Central America, but it wasn't really that. It was the absolute knowledge that God was in control, that he was protecting me, and that my safety was his responsibility. I really didn't care one way or the other what happened to me. I would still be Christ's representative even if I got picked up because I knew that I was in the center of God's will. In Puebla, I just knew there was no question—we were not going to turn around and forsake that village."

Step Seven

◄○►

Establish your profile as a Christian.

One day my assistant Johan Compajon and I were having dinner at a restaurant in Manila. Above the clatter of dishes, we could hear the noise of several air conditioners running, but the place was still very hot. Finally Johan called the waiter.

"Doesn't your air conditioner work here?" Johan asked him.

"Yes, sir," he replied with an embarrassed smile. "It is working, but it is not functioning."

Many Christians are like that. We believe in Jesus, go to church regularly, and remain faithful, but we aren't having much impact on the world around us. We work, but we don't function. And yet God has called us to make a difference, to be the salt of the earth.

Similarly many who have reached the sixth step, presence, have not gone any farther. They have physically gone into a pagan setting and perhaps even spread a bit of goodwill, but they have not yet made it known that they are Christians. The problem is that unless we move forward in our evangelistic efforts, we will begin to stagnate. That's why we need to progress from merely being present to actively establishing what I call a *profile*.

By profile I mean that all of us who belong to Jesus Christ will at some point become visible as such. In order for the world to learn who Jesus is, we should come into the open and make ourselves known. We will not all do this in the same way or on the same time schedule, but God himself will engineer each of our circumstances toward that end.

A good example of such profile evangelism is that of Joseph in the book of Genesis. After being sold into slavery in Egypt by his brothers, Joseph held fast to his faith in the God of Israel. His exemplary life led to a position of leadership in Potiphar's estate. Even after being thrown into jail on false charges, Joseph continued to trust God. But it was not until he took the initiative and asked two fellow prisoners about their disturbing dreams that Joseph moved from simply being there as a believer to actually becoming known as a believer.

"Do not interpretations belong to God?" he said to them. "Tell me your dreams" (Genesis 40:8). Later, when Joseph was brought to Pharaoh's attention as a dream interpreter, he quickly gave the credit to God. "I cannot do it," he told Pharaoh, "but God will give Pharaoh the answer he desires" (41:16). From that point on, Joseph was recognized as a follower of God.

Of course, Joseph could never have orchestrated the circumstances in such a supernatural way; only God could have done it. The same is true for us. But Joseph did do one thing that we should emulate: He took the initiative in asking about people's needs and in proposing God as a solution.

Profile evangelism basically means that taking the initiative becomes a way of life. We are proactive rather than reactive, even if we are arrested or imprisoned. The apostle Paul didn't stop being an apostle when he went to prison. He continued to preach and teach and write letters. Think of how thin the New Testament would be if Paul had given up his initiative in jail!

I could tell story after story about my friends in the former Soviet Union who turned prison camps into revival centers. I am reminded of another Joseph—Joseph Bondarenko, the evangelist to Russia who spent a total of nine years in jail for preaching the gospel. During his first three-year term he had led so many of the inmates to Christ that they cheered when he was sent back to serve a second term.

"We were all praying that you would come back to us," they told him. "We needed someone to teach us the Scriptures."

Brother Bondarenko was not content to simply be a Christian in a hostile country. He wanted to be *known* for his faith so that others could come to know Jesus. I believe that God calls each one of us to do the same thing.

Another friend, a Russian Baptist pastor by the name of Klassen, was standing trial for refusing to stop preaching. Throughout the proceedings he boldly testified of his relationship with Christ, answering every question from his accusers with another question about their souls and eternity. At the court sessions so many people accepted Jesus Christ that the chief judge threw everyone out of the courthouse. My friend Klassen was starting a church there! The rest of the trial took place behind closed doors, but the entire Baptist congregation stood outside the window singing hymns of praise. Klassen was greatly encouraged and he continued preaching. This is what happens when we take the next step from being present to establishing a profile.

There's another element to becoming known for our faith, and it's found at the end of Joseph's story in Genesis 47. After Joseph relocates his family to Egypt, he brings his father before Pharaoh. There, according to the story, Jacob "blessed" Pharaoh. Isn't that what the Christian life should be about—passing on blessings to others whether they be Christians or not? God has called us to be a blessing to the world, a light in the darkness, the salt of the earth.

Keep in mind, however, that when Jesus says we are the salt of the earth, he is not talking about numbers or statistics. Establishing a profile does not necessarily mean becoming the majority. Rather, Jesus is talking about our *influence* on the world.

In spite of all the reports I've heard about the millions of souls we are winning around the world, and the projections that we will be able to reach every person on earth with the gospel by the year 2000, the Christian church seems to have less influence on society than at any time in its history. So rather than fuss over numbers, let us focus instead on backing up our words with the kind of life that others recognize as belonging to Jesus Christ. With that kind of profile, we can bring about real change in the world.

PRAYER

Lord, help me to live in such a way
that your presence in my life is seen by others.
Make me to be a blessing to someone today.
Amen.

Chapter Nine

◄O►

Winds of Change

Nearly twenty years after I had that incredible experience crossing into Czechoslovakia, we were still smuggling Bibles into Eastern Europe and Russia. God was always with us, and I can tell you dozens of stories of his deliverance of our teams from the eyes of searching border guards. *Still,* I thought, *wouldn't it be wonderful if we could do it openly? Probably eighty million Christians in the Soviet Union had no Bible. Why should they have no Bible when I am able to have many Bibles in many different translations? It wasn't fair!*

God, give me an idea, I asked. And as I prayed I saw truckloads of Bibles flowing into the Soviet Union. Border guards tried to stop us, but we said, "We come in the name of Jesus—you cannot stop us."

God was giving me a picture—a vision—of what he would do. I felt so sure of it that I announced it one day in a sermon I preached in Holland.

"Andrew, how can you say that!" my coworkers told me afterward. They were angry that I would make such a statement publicly.

"Because I see it," I said. Of course, I had no idea how God would bring about a Bible delivery of that magnitude, but I knew it would happen somehow.

At that time Open Doors, in partnership with Christians around the world, was in the midst of a prayer campaign for the Soviet Union. The idea had arisen the year before when one of our regional directors had told me of a vision. He had said that God wanted Open Doors to trust God for a delivery of seven million Bibles to the Soviets. I took his words seriously because he was a man of vision. But recalling the immense proportions of Project Pearl, I knew seven million was an awesome number.

"Tell you what," I said to him. "Before we think about seven million Bibles, let's pray for seven years."

It was sort of an offhand remark. But then it occurred to us all that a long-term period of focused prayer might lead to the breakthrough we were looking for behind the Iron Curtain. So we decided to set up a worldwide prayer chain involving every Open Doors office and thousands of our friends and supporters. We called it Seven Years of Prayer for the Soviet Union.

From the years 1984 to 1990, these prayer chains worked around the clock so that prayers were going up to God twenty-four hours a day, seven days a week. We prayed for boldness for the Soviet Christians, unity between Christians of various churches and denominations, and openness to the good news among non-Christians, atheists, and Muslims. Remember, at that time no one had even heard of Gorbachev or *glasnost.* The Cold War was still going on. Leonid Brezhnev had just died, and in 1983 and 1984 he had been followed by hard-liners Yuri Andropov and Konstantin Chernenko. No one knew what to expect.

In those seven years of prayer, everything changed.

Only two years into the campaign a major upheaval in the

Soviet Union became apparent. All of a sudden, it seemed, the winds of change were blowing. Mikhail Gorbachev had come into power and brought a more tolerant policy toward Western ideas, including Christianity. Terms we had never heard before such as *perestroika* and *glasnost* became household words. Who would have dreamed that such dramatic changes would take place in just a few years?

Of course, there was a long way to go before real change would take place. Virtually all of the antireligion laws enacted by Stalin remained in force, and it was still nearly impossible to buy, sell, or distribute the Scriptures freely. Many Christians continued to suffer in Soviet prisons.

But I reminded myself that any time Christians begin to pray in a concentrated way for something, we enter into a real spiritual battle. The enemy intensifies his efforts to defeat us. And believe me, we experienced many attacks during those seven years.

For example, in 1986, the Soviet and East German secret police forces, KGB and Stasi, drew up a five-year plan to infiltrate a number of Christian organizations, including Open Doors, that in their words "operate under a religious cover to undermine socialist nations." The plan was signed by KGB Head Viktor Tshebrikov and Stasi Chief Erich Mielke. Their goal, according to the plan, was to "demask the subversive character" of the organizations and, I imagine, link them to the intelligence activity of NATO countries.

We were doing nothing of the kind, of course, and among our small Dutch and European staff, who prayed and worshiped as well as worked together, I am certain that there were no communist infiltrators. We did not even learn of the plot until years later, but it certainly served to remind us of the dark forces we were up against.

Throughout the early- and mid-1980s, however, we were clearly experiencing setbacks in our smuggling operations. A number of our courier teams were arrested and their Bibles confiscated.

One team, a married couple, had planned a three-week trip to Kiev and then Moscow. Their car pulled a camping trailer with a substantial supply of Scriptures hidden in special compartments.

The timing of their journey turned out to be significant—June 1986, just two months after the nuclear disaster at Chernobyl. As a result, nearly all European tourists heading to Russia had canceled their holidays. So when the couple arrived at the Uzhgorod border station, they realized they were the only ones crossing that day.

The border officials, having nothing else to do, decided to question the couple at length and conduct a thorough search of the car and trailer. After four hours of waiting and answering questions, the pair were suddenly ushered to their car. There another stern-faced official showed them a hole about four centimeters wide that he had drilled in the floor of the vehicle. Shreds of paper had come out when he removed the drill—Bible paper.

"Either cooperate and help your case by opening your storage system," the guard demanded, "or else we will break it apart." Reluctantly the husband opened the panels. With a sense of triumph, the officials gathered around to uncover the entire load of Scriptures.

More waiting. Soon several photographers arrived with video equipment. The couple were forced to reenact the entire approach to the border for the cameras. After that humiliating ordeal, they were taken to a nearby hotel by KGB agents.

"But before you go to your room," the agent in charge said, "let's have a little talk."

A difficult two-hour interrogation followed. Fortunately the couple had been briefed thoroughly, and they shared their "cover story," basically a general description of their holiday plans that also included some Christian testimony. The agent refused to believe them and warned them to come up with a better story when he returned the next morning.

The couple had trouble sleeping that night, as you can imagine. They prayed to God for guidance and protection, but mostly they struggled with frustration, disappointment, uncertainty, and fear. Why did this happen? And what about all the prayers others had offered for their safety? Didn't they make any difference?

On Sunday the grueling interrogations continued. No violence or physical force was used, and the Lord gave them the grace and the strength not to divulge the names and specifics of Open Doors or the people they had intended to meet.

Later that day they were sent back to their room, discouraged and exhausted, where they could only pray, wait, and wonder what would happen next. To pass the time, they decided to listen to Russian radio.

Then an amazing thing happened. The deep, soulful sound of African American spirituals filled the room—the last thing you'd expect to hear on the government-run radio stations of Russia. The words to the very first song were, "Nobody knows the trouble I have seen, nobody knows but Jesus; sometimes I'm up, sometimes I'm down, nobody knows but Jesus."

How true that song was, and how perfectly it captured their feelings! That very moment they felt God speaking to them. Through that spiritual he was saying, "I am with you all the way. I have seen your obedience and that's what matters most. I will take care of the rest." Tears came to their eyes at the gentle reminder of God's presence.

From then on, their confidence and their boldness grew. On Monday morning, as they continued to wait in their room for some word from officials, they sang and worshiped the Lord for an hour and a half. After lunch a journalist from the communist youth paper *Komsomolskaya Pravda* came to interview them—

perhaps to get more information, or more likely to use the couple's experience for propaganda purposes.

His first question: "What is the greatest need of the youth in Holland?"

The husband thought for a moment, then knew exactly what to say. "The need of Holland's youth is the very same as that of Russian youth," he said. "They both need Jesus Christ!" For the rest of the interview, they answered questions by sharing their testimony and the gospel message.

At 4:30 P.M. they were taken back to the border again, where they stood before a tribunal of many border officials. They were told that their car, trailer, and all their literature had been confiscated, and that they had exactly one hour to pack their remaining personal belongings. Amid taunts and jeers from the guards, the couple stuffed their clothing, food, and other effects into ten plastic bags, which they had to lug to a waiting bus headed back into Czechoslovakia.

In exchange for their food, the bus driver helped them purchase a ticket for the overnight train to Bratislava, near the Austrian border. Finally they reached Vienna, where they had an emotional phone call with a colleague. As it turned out, another team had also been arrested at a different border. Apparently something bigger was going on than a random search of a vehicle.

I am happy to say that the couple still work and are more determined than ever to serve the suffering church. They told me that their three days of humiliation and inconvenience were nothing compared to the suffering of many Soviet Christians in prisons and labor camps.

And the overwhelming majority of our courier runs were successful—that is, the Bibles were delivered safely. For every team that was caught, fifty others made it through.

Another coworker, who has also been arrested, gained a new perspective on the worldwide body of Christians while successfully delivering a consignment of two thousand Bibles to East Germany. Unbeknownst to him, his contact, who was recovering from an illness, had visited nearby relatives for the weekend, so no one was home when the courier team arrived to make delivery arrangements. The next day the team returned, and the contact's daughter, who was in her twenties, answered the door.

"Come in," she said. "We are expecting you. We were away so Father could rest and have a change of pace, but at two o'clock this afternoon the Lord told us to go home. We arrived thirty minutes ago."

With warmth and tenderness in his eyes, the grateful contact began to explain how to reach the rendezvous point for the Bible delivery. My colleague could see right away that his friend did not realize the load was too big for a single drop-off. A car would be needed to transfer the boxes of Scriptures back and forth from the large van to the storage location.

"Brother," he interrupted the contact, "we will have to do this three times." He said it reluctantly, as if his contact might decline a three-stage delivery because of the greater risk.

To the contrary, the man's eyes brightened. "Fantastic," he said.

The transfer took place without a hitch. At the completion of the third drop, the team was about to leave when the contact said these remarkable words: "When you return home, please tell all those Christians who gave sacrificially to provide these Scriptures that we all belong to one circle of love. When we cannot come to say thank-you ourselves, the Lord Jesus will come to them and thank them on our behalf and so complete the circle for us."

◄o►

Meanwhile, as our seven-year prayer campaign continued, I became acquainted with a prominent Dutch businessman who I understood was doing some kind of work in Russia. I had known of him for years through his younger brother, who at that time worked for the Dutch Bible Society. I finally contacted him because I thought he might be able to help us set up trucking or importing businesses in Russia that we could use to deliver Bibles. I was still trying to think of ways we could sneak in.

He explained to me that he doesn't conduct any business in Russia at all, but only travels there in an unofficial capacity. As I got to know this fascinating man, who was also a dedicated Christian, I realized he was indeed something of a self-styled diplomat. Over the years he had developed relationships with past and present governmental leaders of many countries—ambassadors, generals, members of Congress and Parliament, cabinet members, presidents, and prime ministers. Why did he do this? Because as a Christian, he wanted to use his influence to help solve world problems and resolve conflicts through peaceful, behind-the-scenes negotiation. He knew how to bring people together unofficially in a neutral setting, making it possible to deal with issues quickly and candidly while bypassing the rhetoric and red tape of official politics.

I liked the man's style a great deal since I, too, prefer to work behind the scenes. I'm much more interested in having influence than in getting credit.

One day in early 1987 he invited me to visit him at his estate near the coast in Holland. He wanted to talk to me about an intriguing request he had received from the European Security Council. They wanted him to arrange a human rights conference between the Soviet Union and the United States. The group would be a non-governmental organization (NGO), which means that all attendees participate only as private citizens, not as official representatives of their countries. The tone of the conference would be nonconfrontational, and publicity would be kept to a minimum.

"The Soviets are suggesting a conference where the countries can discuss present and upcoming problems," he told me. (Later

I realized they were anticipating the breakdown of the Iron Curtain even before we had thought of it.) "What I'm wondering, Andrew, is whether you and Open Doors would be willing to organize it."

I could hardly believe my ears. "What do you mean by organizing it?"

"Well," he said, "I'm basically asking if you could handle everything except choosing the delegates and planning the program. You would coordinate all the logistics—conference facilities, food, lodging, transportation and security for all the guests, and any other necessary details. In addition, you would represent the Netherlands at the conference. Can you do it?"

I had no idea. But since I never say no to an extraordinary opportunity, I went back to Johan and another colleague, Evert, and told them about my meeting. I'll probably never know what really went through their minds when I asked them to put together a proposal, but if they were thinking, *Oh no, here we go again, Andrew,* they didn't say it.

A few weeks later, the three of us returned to my friend's house to present the proposal. We weren't just showing it to him, however; several top Soviet officials had flown in for the presentation. I tell you, the entire time we met, a million thoughts and feelings raced through my head. There we were, three renegade Bible smugglers, having dinner with Communist Party leaders and planning a conference together! Evert and Johan gave a flawless presentation and made a positive impression on everyone, so we were approved as the conference organizers. Evert assumed primary responsibility for all conference logistics.

What a monumental task he had—and what a marvelous job he did at keeping track of countless details and arrangements. The whole thing finally came off on January 4 to 6, 1988, at the De Burght Christian Conference Center in the Dutch province of Zeeland. We called it the Conference on Human Rights and International Cooperation.

I was amazed at the roster of distinguished participants, primarily from the Soviet Union and the United States, but also from a number of Eastern and Western European countries. There were about fifty people in all—conservative and liberal political leaders, Protestant, Catholic, and Russian Orthodox religious leaders, and a variety of other academicians and experts on international affairs. Especially notable delegates included Rosalynn Carter, wife of the former U.S. president; Mrs. Giscard d' Estaing, wife of the former president of France; Fyodor Burlatsky, chairman of the Soviet Commission on Humanitarian Problems and Human Rights and a close adviser to Mikhail Gorbachev; Alexander Sukharev, minister of justice of the Russian Republic; Landrum Bolling, president of the Ecumenical Institute in Jerusalem; Patrick Cormack, member of the British Parliament; Theodore Hesburgh, president emeritus of the University of Notre Dame in Indiana; American theologian Richard Neuhaus; and a number of present and former members of the U.S. Congress.

I was most interested in the Soviet delegation, of course, because they had the power to influence current policies on the right of Russian Christians to worship freely and obtain Bibles. With those people especially in mind, I set up tables throughout the conference center stacked with free Bibles and Christian books—including *God's Smuggler.* I wanted them to take lots of books home with them, which they did.

At one point a KGB member who had been perusing the book tables asked me to sign a copy of *Building in a Broken World,* my book on leadership.

"I'd be happy to," I said to him, pulling out my pen. "And if you like," I added with a smile, "I could even sign my other book, *God's Smuggler.*"

"There is no need for that," he said wryly. "We all have that book on our shelves in Moscow."

During the whole conference, I couldn't stop thinking about

two things: the great need for Russian Bibles, and the list we carried with us of four hundred prisoners, many of whom were Christians, still languishing in Soviet labor camps and psychiatric institutions. I and many other Western delegates were determined to address both issues with the Soviet officials. But how? And what would I say?

One evening at dinner, Dr. Burlatsky and I were talking about our backgrounds and about religious freedom, and he said something that I thought I would never hear from a Communist Party leader.

"If only we could go back to the simplicity of the faith as we have heard it from Moses and Jesus," he said.

It was so true, not only for the Soviet Union but for every country. At that moment I believe the Lord confirmed in my heart a wild idea I had been thinking about for some time. Why not offer the Russian Orthodox Church an official gift of one million Bibles? After all, I had been pondering a passage in the Psalms that said, "Forever, O LORD, your word is settled in heaven." If that is indeed the case, then it occurred to me that the Bible must also be forever available on earth. And what better time to offer than now, since 1988 was the year the Russian Orthodox Church was celebrating its one thousandth birthday?

I remembered a trip I'd made to the Soviet Union in 1967, when a Russian Orthodox priest had come to me and said, "Why do you always give your Bibles to the Baptists? We too need Scriptures." I had no answer for him. We had overlooked the possibility. The Orthodox have many martyrs and many brave believers. Some of them worshiped with Baptist preachers in the same prison camps.

Similarly I have a Jesuit friend from America who had wanted to be a missionary in Siberia. Years ago he had gone to Russia, preached the gospel, and was arrested. He had spent his first five years in solitary confinement in Moscow, and then nineteen years in the gulags of—where else—Siberia. Eventually he had been released in exchange for two Russian spies the Americans had caught in New York.

When I had spoken to him after his release, the first thing he had said to me was, "Andrew, in those twenty-four years, I was not sick even one day." Clearly the Catholic brother had been there under divine protection. His experience reminded me that the needs of the suffering church extend to those in official church bodies as well.

So at one point later in the conference I stood up and said, "I want to make a little speech." Everyone looked at me, and I admit I was nervous. I was going to offer to do something that had never been done in the entire history of Russia. The Bible had been forbidden even before the Bolshevik Revolution, and since then almost all Bibles that were discovered by the authorities had been destroyed. How could I make such an offer now? I didn't know, but I believed God wanted me to do it. I also sensed that in the setting, it would be hard for the Russian church or government to refuse.

I said a quiet prayer in my heart, and I decided to start with a story. I told them about my visit to the SWAPO guerrilla headquarters in Angola—the visit I described in chapter five of this book—and my discussion with the Marxist leader about placing a Bible on his desk next to the bust of Lenin.

I repeated the same statement I had made to that guerrilla leader, that no nation can be happy when its people are forced to live under a political or religious system that they have not chosen. The same was true for the Soviet people, I said. They can never be happy unless they have access to the alternative to communism—Jesus Christ. Everyone present knew I was the Bible smuggler. I mean, on every book table I had piles of copies of *God's Smuggler* as well as my other books, and I made it no secret that I was totally devoted to getting the Scriptures into Russia.

"And I will continue to take Bibles to Russia in whatever way I can," I went on, "until everyone in the church has a Bible, until everyone in the school has a Bible, and until the Bible is available in all the bookshops so that people can simply walk in and buy the Word of God."

As I spoke what must have sounded like outrageous words, the Soviets in the conference room were speechless. But I had gotten that far; there could be no turning back.

"Therefore as a beginning," I said, "I am now offering a gift of one million Bibles to the Russian Orthodox Church."

There—I said it. I must admit I hadn't discussed it with my board of directors because they probably would have voted against it. Sometimes there are things you must do when God tells you to and leave the consequences up to him.

I also referred to those four hundred prisoners, and I urged the Soviet leaders to unconditionally release them all. "As long as there is one prisoner in Russia for his faith in Jesus," I said, "then I am not free! We will not stop when *most* of the prisoners have been released and Open Doors will not stop when a *great many* Bibles have been provided. No, we shall go on until *every* prisoner has been released and until *everyone* who wants a Bible has access to one." Of course, I was not the only one to talk about the prisoners; another delegate later made an eloquent appeal, after which he handed the complete list of Christian prisoners to the minister of justice.

After my speech it was time for a break. As we stood up and moved toward the table where coffee was being served, a pleasant-looking gentleman walked up.

"Andrew," he said, "I kind of like you, but I did not like your speech."

I looked at his name tag. He was Marian Dobrosielsky, a Polish government official, which at that time was still under communist rule.

"Answer me one question," he continued. "If I came into one

of your buildings and on every desk I saw a Bible, would you let me put a statue of Lenin next to it?"

It was another one of those situations when you have no time for prayer. Yet in that split second while he looked at me, anxiously waiting for my answer, God revealed something terrific to me: *If people have access to the Bible and if they truly base their lives upon it, then let Lenin come. He will come anyway, or else someone like him. Let temptation come. Let sin come. Let problems come. Let anything come. If my life is grounded firmly upon the Word of God, then in Christ I am more than a conqueror.*

"Yes," I said, "I would let you do that."

Immediately his face relaxed into a smile, and he grabbed my hand warmly. "Now," he said, "we are real friends." And from that day on we have kept in touch with each other.

The conference ended with an official reception at the Ministry of State Department in The Hague. Response to my offer had been generally positive, though I would not know for months whether it would be officially accepted. Metropolitan Juvenaly, head of foreign affairs for the Russian Orthodox Church, issued a tentative statement: "It is possible to import Bibles that are offered to us by various churches."

Burlatsky, however, applauded the offer. "I see no problem whatsoever," he said in a press conference afterward. "The Bible is not only a religious book, but a book of great cultural and moral value. I myself have a Bible at home."

Even a KGB general by the name of Andrei Grachev came up to me as we were saying good-bye. He shook my hand and said, "Andrew, you are very welcome with your million Bibles, but please don't do it all in one night like you did in China."

I laughed. "Don't worry, Andrei. I won't. I won't."

◄o►

I half expected my staff and the Open Doors board of directors to shake their heads after hearing of my million-Bible offer to the Russian church—especially after I'd done it without con-sulting them first. But they "forgave" me and wholeheartedly gave their support to the idea. We simply needed to wait for the church's answer.

It came in the form of a request from one of the church lead-ers. He asked that I repeat my offer to them in writing. Then he added, somewhat apologetically, "Instead of offering us com-plete Bibles, would you be willing to change your offer to New Testaments with Psalms? Most of our people would not know how to handle the Old Testament."

So I sent an official letter to Patriarch Pimen, the spiritual leader of the entire Russian Orthodox Church. The letter read in part:

This year's historic celebration of the millennium of Chris-tianity in Russia is an important milestone in the worldwide history of Christianity. As members of one church in Christ, we know that the one unifying factor to our faith is found in the pages of the Word of God—the Holy Bible.

In keeping with the Spirit of the millennial celebration and our desire in the West to join with you during this historic moment, it is my privilege and honor to represent many Christian organizations in offering the Russian Orthodox Church a gift of one million New Testaments with Psalms to be delivered during 1988.

Unfortunately we did not get a reply for some time, and our anticipation was replaced by concern and then worry. Two, three, four months went by. Were they not going to accept after all? Or had my request been buried in a sea of socialist red tape? I shot off several more letters to the church and to a Soviet official from the conference who worked for the Council on Religious Problems. Still nothing.

In mid-July, a letter finally arrived at my office from Metropolitan Filaret, chairman of the Russian Orthodox Church Department for External Church Relations:

> It is with great gratitude that we received your letter. . . . We would like to thank you sincerely for this lavish expression of Christian love and consider it a pleasant duty to inform you that we have agreed to accept the edition of the Holy Scriptures offered to us. . . .

> With cordial greetings in the Lord and best wishes for good progress in your labours.

What a time of rejoicing we had that day! Just as history had been made in China by the Project Pearl delivery of a million Bibles, it was about to be made again in Russia. Excitedly I sent back a letter of confirmation:

> It brings much joy to hear that you are cooperating with Western Christians to distribute these Scriptures among the Russian Orthodox believers of the Soviet Union.

> We are proceeding with the printing of the first 100,000 New Testaments and anticipate their delivery before Christmas. . . . I would appreciate it if you could arrange for you and I to meet on the delivery of this first shipment.

A million New Testaments, one hundred thousand at a time, pouring into Russia—openly, even officially. Who could have imagined it? But then I remembered the vision God had given me, the image of truckloads of Scriptures passing freely across Soviet borders. Barely a year after I saw that vision, it was all coming true.

Step Eight

◄o►

Become part of a permanent presence wherever you are.

In *God's Smuggler* I told about visiting a tiny remote village in what used to be Yugoslavia. Together with a good friend who spoke the local language, we drove in my Volkswagen and watched the road change from pavement to dirt, from dirt to a pair of ruts, and finally from ruts to a freshly plowed field. Then we got out and traipsed through the fields until we reached the little community of Nosaki.

There in that village on the edge of nowhere we found the house of an old, poor woman, Anna. On the whitewashed facade of her home, she had painted two words in large black letters: MOLITVEN DOM, house of prayer. The phrase originally came from Isaiah 56:7, and was quoted by Jesus in Matthew 21:13: "My house will be called a house of prayer." Anna had moved beyond the stage of being known as a Christian; she had established a place where believers could meet and pray. That's what step eight is all about—putting down roots, setting up a permanent base of operations.

Throughout my days of traveling in Eastern Europe, when I would go into a town and ask where the church was, people would usually shrug their shoulders and say they didn't know. But if I asked, "Where is the house of prayer?" they would say, "Oh, yes—here are the directions."

Once we become visible as a Christian witness in an area—and we are living out our faith in a genuine, active way—the result will be a gathering of local believers. I am not speaking of physical structures or building programs, but I am talking about a *place*—a place that is known as the house of the Lord. It may be no more than the living room of one family's home, but it is a place where people meet in the name of Jesus Christ.

What is the key to this step of permanence? Christians who are willing to go to a place of God's calling and *stay* there. Of course, I support all the wonderful opportunities people have for short-term mission service, especially among young people. It gives them a great experience and a taste of what cross-cultural evangelism is like. But then they go home before learning the language and the culture from the inside. I fear that if we overemphasize the short-term approach, we will develop a hit-and-run attitude toward missions. Too many groups have made the missionary call too cheap. God wants our whole lives. There is a price to be paid. And that means more than visiting a place temporarily to carry out a project or sponsor a big campaign.

God wants people who will serve him over the long haul. Again I return to Joseph in the book of Genesis. When he arrived in Egypt after being sold into slavery, I believe he had no thought of ever returning home. Somehow he knew he would live in the foreign land for the rest of his life. Why did he not try to escape and go back to his family? Because he believed that

God had placed him in Egypt for a purpose. (We see this later when in Genesis 45:5 he tells his brothers, "It was to save lives that God sent me ahead of you.") So instead of running away, Joseph accepted where God had put him, settled in Egypt, and at that point moved into step eight, the permanent stage of evangelism.

As a result of his commitment to stay, Joseph did indeed preserve life. God was with him and blessed him until eventually he became the second most powerful man in Egypt. Through his wise management of food resources during a famine, he saved many lives and later would even save his own family from starvation. But it never would have happened had he not remained in Egypt.

Staying in one place for the sake of the kingdom may mean different things for different people. For a missionary, it usually means going to live and make a home in a foreign country. But think about the many movements of refugees around the world —from Bosnia, from Cuba, from Haiti, from China. (Or consider entire nations of people who have no country, such as the Palestinians and the Kurds.) Refugees usually do not look back; they're too focused on surviving and starting a new life. However, I would implore Christians among these peoples to consider training and equipping themselves to return to their home countries as servants of Jesus.

Or think of the millions of Christians who have lived under an oppressive communist system for many years and now have the freedom to emigrate to the West if they wish. I understand their desire to have a better life, to leave a land of poverty for a land of opportunity. But I still pray with all my heart that they will choose to stay (or else seek biblical training and then return) and use their newfound freedom to build the kingdom of God right where they are.

Or what about the well-known dissidents from Russia and

other repressive regimes? Many of them had a tremendous influence on the church and even society at large while they were in prison. But what happened to them once they were released? Aleksandr Solzhenitsyn moved to America, became a millionaire, made a couple of good speeches while the people were still listening, and then lost his influence. I'm glad that he has now returned to Russia, but I fear his opportunity to make a real difference there may have passed.

I've always encouraged newly released Christian prisoners not to emigrate to or travel extensively in the West, but to consider how God could use them even more effectively in their home country. The fall of communism was a good thing, but it only revealed how great the spiritual needs are in those nations. Who is better equipped to take the initiative and meet those needs than a Christian leader who knows the people and the language and has suffered for his or her faith?

Starting a church in a closed country is not easy. That place, and those who go there, will probably be targeted for persecution by the government or some other group. They might burn down the building, kill the pastor, pressure the young people, and more. Persecution and suffering will very likely be a part of the picture. But at least a local house of the Lord will be functioning.

The house church movement in China is probably the greatest movement of the Holy Spirit since Pentecost. Conservative estimates of Chinese believers in house churches number around sixty million. All this growth happened during and after Mao's Cultural Revolution. These churches have no denominations, no buildings, no ordained priests, no music directors, no television evangelists. And yet they thrive because dedicated Christians were determined to establish a "house of prayer" where believers could gather regularly.

PRAYER

Lord, you have called me for a purpose.
Wherever you lead me, help me to stay there and serve you
faithfully.
Amen.

Chapter Ten

◄○►

From
Hammer and Sickle
to
Hammer and Chisel

*F*rom the time I received that letter of acceptance from the Russian Orthodox Church, events seemed to accelerate rapidly —in Russia, in Eastern Europe, and in Open Doors.

Only a few months later—January 1989—I found myself on an airplane headed for Moscow. The trip would be unlike any I had ever made to the Soviet Union. For one thing, it was my first trip to the country in more than twenty years. To protect the many contacts I had there, I had never been back after the publication of *God's Smuggler*. But I was not only back—I was an invited guest!

The De Burght human rights group, as we called it, was having a follow-up meeting in Moscow. That in itself demonstrated how much things had changed. But there had been other hopeful signs. Through our various information channels, we had learned that nearly all of the prisoners mentioned at the first conference had been set free. No announcements had been made. No laws were changed. The dissidents were simply let go. (The last few remaining prisoners were more complicated cases and their release was imminent.) Word reached us later that the De Burght group had been largely responsible for their release—though, of course, I knew that it never would have happened without the prayers of thousands of believers around the world.

As my flight descended into Moscow's Sheremetyevo International Airport, I maintained a little healthy skepticism about the situation there. After all, the Soviet Union was still very much a union, and its Communist system and top-heavy bureaucracy remained in place—for the time being at least. But the positive developments I had witnessed, the official acceptance of a million New Testaments, and now an authorized meeting with government leaders gave me a real feeling of excitement.

I even excused the airport officials when they apologetically informed me that my luggage—which included two large boxes of Bibles—had been misplaced. But there were no suspicious looks and no interrogations to endure. All I had to do was show my passport. Since I was part of the human-rights conference, I was met by three men—a guide, an interpreter, and a chauffeur—who for the next few days literally gave me the "red" carpet treatment.

They took me to the Party Hotel, an exquisite first-class facility in central Moscow, where I met up with some of the other participants. It was a new feeling to be an honored guest in a communist country—an uncomfortable feeling actually because I'm more accustomed to being treated like a criminal!

At the first break in our meetings, I went for a walk in Red Square. In a way it looked just as I remembered it. Other than the majestic onion domes of St. Basil's Cathedral, the square was drab and dirty. And yet in another way it seemed completely different. I noticed a drastic reduction in the number of soldiers and guns. The atmosphere was more relaxed, more upbeat. People were selling things on the sidewalks. Street musicians performed on the corners. More of the faces had smiles on them. The shift toward a free-market economy, and especially toward freedom, was happening right before my eyes.

I felt like I was walking through a dream. There I was, moving about freely in the spiritual center of the communist world, a center that could no longer hold. I thought of all the prayers that had been said, all the Bibles our teams had brought in, all the believers in that country who had suffered in the hope that the oppression of this system would one day come to an end. And though the end had not yet arrived, and there would still be much upheaval and instability over the next few years, I knew that day would be coming soon. *I am probably the happiest missionary in the world,* I thought, *because I am seeing my dreams come true.* In a couple of months I would be personally presenting the first of a million New Testaments to the Russian Orthodox Church in an official, government-sanctioned ceremony. It amazed me to realize I didn't have to smuggle Scriptures there anymore.

Speaking of Scriptures, two days had gone by and I still had not received my luggage. I had sent someone from the hotel to the airport each day to check on it until finally on the third day he came back with my suitcase, but no Bibles. No one at the airport seemed to know where the two boxes of Bibles were, the man said.

Something's wrong here, I said to myself. My healthy skepticism reminded me that the system hadn't completely changed yet. I just knew that the minute I checked in for my return flight to Amsterdam, they would suddenly, inexplicably find my Bibles.

The human-rights conference went smoothly. We discussed the many changes that had taken place since our last meeting, and we learned that the Soviets were in the process of writing new laws on religious freedom. Our input into that process would be helpful.

I gave a little speech about the Russian church's acceptance of my offer of one million New Testaments. And while we were there at the conference, I officially gave Fyodor Burlatsky a nice Russian Bible. He was one of the most influential men in the Soviet Union at that time—one of Gorbachev's special advisers. It was incredible to see how God's Word could reach into the highest levels of Russian leadership. He gratefully accepted it, but I was unprepared for his wonderful response.

"Andrew," he said, "this is already the third Bible I have received this year. The first one, my wife confiscated. I will never see it anymore because she reads it day and night. Then somebody else gave me a Bible, but my son took it away from me. I'll never see that one anymore, either. But, Andrew, now I have my own personal copy. This I will keep."

When the time came to return to Holland, I purposely checked in early because I wanted to retrieve those Bibles. I was determined not to take them home with me. With my interpreter, guide, and driver at my side, I went to the Lost and Found department, a huge warehouse, and asked about my boxes.

"No problem, sir," the official said, "your boxes are right over here on the desk."

Just as I thought.

"What's in here?" he said to me.

"Bibles for the church," I replied, somewhat impatiently.

I suppose I had to experience one last round of red tape before leaving. They sent me to their superior, who told me to fill out a batch of long forms describing all the contents, what my itinerary had been, and so on. And no one was guaranteeing that I'd get my boxes back. After pleading with the officials in Lost and Found and getting nowhere, in total exasperation I did something I would normally never do—I resorted to name-dropping.

"Well, one thing I can say for sure—my friend Alexander Sukharev, the minister of justice, won't like this one bit."

Not even a minute later I was walking out of Lost and Found with my boxes of Bibles. I did not have to sign a single piece of paper or speak to another person. I tell you, the whole Soviet system was based on who you knew.

I handed the boxes of Bibles to my driver and said, "Please take these to the Baptist church. Here's the address." Then I got onto my flight back to Amsterdam.

—◄o►—

The first shipment of one hundred thousand New Testaments arrived in Moscow during the first week of December 1988, just in time to close out the Russian Orthodox Church's millennial year. The ceremony in which I officially presented the "first" Bible took place on January 13, 1989, in the partially restored Danilov Monastery. The beautiful old facility, which serves as the Russian church's headquarters, had been confiscated by the communists during Stalin's rule and only recently had been given back.

A variety of priests, metropolitans, and members of the monastery staff had been invited to the evening presentation. It was such a momentous occasion for me and I was so nervous that when it was time for me to speak, I addressed the group as "dear extinguished guests." But I quickly corrected myself and went on to tell them what was on my heart.

I said that the New Testaments were a gift from Christians in the West to mark the millennium of the Russian Orthodox Church. I also spoke of the gifts the Russian church had to offer to the West—their love, their faith, and their endurance.

"It is my earnest desire to have a vital link with the Russian church," I said. "This is only a small gift that we can give to you. We want to do more, but above all we want the fellowship of the saints because this precious Word of God is written for everyone in the world, to teach us the way of God."

After I spoke, several church leaders came forward to respond. Archbishop Iov said, "On behalf of the people of our church, I would like to thank you for this gift to our church, for your love to our church and to our church members. I would like to assure you that this New Testament will really get to the believers and it will have a place of honor in their homes and in their lives."

Then another priest, Father Vitali Borovoi, offered thanks on behalf of the monks of the monastery and the staff of the Department for External Church Relations: "You call yourselves Open Doors and that is just what is needed, both for us here and also for you in the West. So the doors are gradually opening in our country and in yours, but they don't open easily because they have been closed for a long time. Humanity was divided and was not willing to acknowledge each other as they did battle with each other. Now the door has opened so that we can look at each other and cooperate with each other."

Then Father Borovoi went on to give a striking bit of Russian church history that I'd never heard before. "[The millennium of our church] is the occasion for the gift, but it is a very symbolic occasion. This is because of the brother who has offered the gift —Andrew."

He turned and pointed to a large painting on the wall behind him. "Christianity in our country," he continued, "was introduced by the apostle Andrew. You can see him there in that painting. According to tradition, he was the first to come to Russia in order to preach the gospel of our Lord. Our church considers itself to be the church of the apostle Andrew. He brought Christianity to the Greek-Roman world, and you, with your books and activities, are a continuation of that apostleship. The acts of the apostle Andrew go on, and this is a continuation that we welcome in our country.

"However . . . it is not only you and our Western brothers who must print these New Testaments and distribute them here. I think it is our task—the most important task of our church—to continue and to print Bibles ourselves. We have done it six times, but that was not sufficient for the fifty million Bibles that our people need. This is our clear duty and task because without this, because without [the Bible], our church, which is so rich in spirituality, would not be a church."

What a great story! I especially appreciated his final comments because they highlight what I see as my calling and the purpose of Open Doors. Our job is not to do for others what they can do for themselves, but to support and strengthen the church so it can carry on its own work of spreading the faith. I want to open the door the first time, and then let others walk through it.

After all the formalities, I started handing out New Testaments to the priests and to the monastery staff. The response was overwhelming. One priest asked for a thousand copies. I told him no problem, but we'd have to ship them separately. Whatever they asked for, we would find a way to do it.

One of the monks said, "Andrew, you shouldn't just do this here, but also in the churches so that the ordinary people get a Bible, too."

Two days later, while I attended more meetings of the human-rights group, two of my Open Doors colleagues did just that—they visited the Elijah Church in Moscow, where they were able to hand out two hundred New Testaments. Members of the congregation surged to the front of the church in hopes of receiving a copy, and many recipients could not hold back their tears of joy.

My entire visit with the Russian Orthodox Church leaders was a wonderful time to make friends with Christian brothers we'd had virtually no contact with before. Up to that point, most of our contacts had been Baptists and other evangelicals. The Baptists never held it against us, and we made sure they got their share of Bibles as well.

─◄o►─

I made several trips to Russia over the next year or so, and each time, it seemed, I had a new experience or heard a new report that indicated real change was taking place in the communist world.

On my second visit, I made sure my luggage didn't get lost again, and I took a more aggressive stance on bringing in Bibles. At the customs desk, I plopped down my two boxes in front of the official and said, "These are Bibles—open them and I'll show you."

Somewhat taken aback, the official refused to open my boxes. Perhaps she thought I'd start preaching at her, I'm not sure—but she allowed me to bring them right in without so much as a signature. Much better!

In addition to meeting with Russian Orthodox Church leaders, I visited a number of evangelical churches that we had supplied with Bibles over the years. Some seemed just the same as I had remembered—the standing congregation filling the sanctuary, the women wearing head scarves, the slow, serious hymn singing in a minor key. The longtime believers had been faithful for many years, and they intended to continue in their faith.

But I also came across Christians who were taking bold new steps to evangelize in their changing country. The Baptist church in Moscow had rented a huge theater and used megaphones to openly invite people on the street to the services. I wanted to see what that meeting was like, so along with two of my colleagues, I went in and sat down.

The large auditorium was packed, and clearly not just with Christians. Most Russian evangelicals and Baptists dressed and behaved very conservatively, and they would never smoke or drink. So I could simply tell by the cigarette smoke and the style of clothing that the believers had succeeded in attracting many non-Christians. I couldn't understand the sermons from the various speakers, but the way they pointed to their Bibles and the spirit in which they spoke and prayed left no doubt that they were clearly preaching the gospel. At the end, an invitation was given and many people raised their hands or came forward to accept Christ. The tremendous response moved me deeply.

After the service we made our way through the crowd until we reached the platform. The leaders and speakers knew who we were and greeted us warmly.

Their first question was, "Andrew, why didn't you hand out Bibles?" They had no Scriptures to offer to the people.

"Dear me, I didn't know we could do that," I replied. The Soviet Union was still very much in transition, and from one month to the next it was not always apparent which activities would be tolerated and which would not. But the fact that Christians were being allowed to hold evangelistic meetings—or do anything Christian, for that matter—outside a church building indicated a significant shift in the political climate. We were seeing it with our own eyes, and that made me very happy.

The change seemed to be spreading beyond Soviet borders as well. I had a funny experience on one of my plane flights back from Moscow when we had to make a stopover in Warsaw. I sat on the aisle, and the two seats to my right were empty. Gradually the plane filled up with passengers until every seat was taken except the two next to me. Finally, after everybody was seated, two men in black suits and clerical collars came down the aisle.

They stopped next to me, checked their boarding passes, and confirmed that the two seats were theirs.

I stood up to let them in and said, "Hello, my name is Brother Andrew."

The first man smiled. "*My* name is Brother Andrew," he replied and sat down. Then, to my utter amazement, the second man said, "My name is also Brother Andrew."

They were both Polish Catholic missionaries to Brazil! And one of them had been involved in the Oasis Movement, a charismatic movement in Poland that Open Doors had supported for years. So there we were, three Brother Andrews in one row. My spirits were lifted, not only by the comical "coincidence," but by the fact that the two men were Christian missionaries sent by the church in a still-communist country. The world was changing indeed.

Another incredible story reached our offices later of a growing Baptist congregation in Kobrin, near the Polish border in what is now the Republic of Belarus. The believers had received a permit to construct their first church building, but the scarcity of materials made it impossible for them to begin. Finally the authorities granted them permission to carry out what only a few years earlier would have been unthinkable. They were allowed to tear down a nearby abandoned Soviet army barracks and missile silo in order to salvage the bricks, concrete blocks, and steel for construction of their church.

While church volunteers were demolishing the site, they uncovered an empty World War II artillery shell sealed within a brick wall. Rolled up inside the shell was a letter, in Russian, written in 1948. It said simply: "These bricks came from Polish Orthodox and Russian Orthodox churches. If this missile complex is ever torn down, we ask that the bricks be used to build churches." It was signed by several people, presumably Christian construction workers.

During and after World War II, Stalin had destroyed many churches and used the materials to build up the Soviet military machine. Now God was allowing the bricks to be restored to their rightful use—for the building of his kingdom. Polish Canadian missionary George Bajenski, who passed on the story, echoed Isaiah 2:4 when he said, "The plowshare was first beaten into a sword, and then back into a plowshare."

With the tragic exception of China's Tiananmen Square massacre in June of 1989, the breezes of democracy and freedom of expression met with little resistance wherever they blew—especially in Russia and Eastern Europe. One by one the Soviet satellite countries declared independence and elected their own leaders. In the Czech Republic, a playwright, Vaclav Havel, was made president. In Romania, the brutal dictator Nicolae Ceausescu was overthrown, and people were seen on the streets of Bucharest tearing out the hammer and sickle from the center of the national flag.

Perhaps the most powerful and symbolic event of all was the breaking down of the Berlin Wall, which divided that city, and seemingly the whole world, into communist and noncommunist camps. Though I was not present for that extraordinary milestone, my colleague, Jan, was present at the December ceremony to open the Wall.

Hundreds of thousands of people had gathered at the Brandenburg Gate, the most infamous point of the Wall. There were emotional reunions between those who had escaped to West Berlin in previous years and their relatives who had been unable to leave. Some had not seen their kinfolk in fifteen or twenty years.

Amid the crowd were some Christians who evangelized using an enormous banner with the words of Psalm 24:7: "Lift up your heads, O you gates . . . that the King of glory may come in." A very appropriate passage for the Brandenburg Gate. It also conveyed a powerful message, as if to say: Peace is not the absence of communism, but the presence of *the* King of glory, Jesus Christ. After the Wall was officially opened, the Christians carried their banner into East Berlin and continued to evangelize—the first time such activity had taken place in many years.

Jan was one of the thousands who actually climbed onto the Wall with a hammer and helped to break it down. He collected pieces of the Wall to give away to friends who had prayed so long and so earnestly for its fall. And when he spoke about his experience later, he said, "The hammer and sickle have given way to the hammer and chisel." I liked that.

I can't say I had any interest in a piece of the Wall for myself. Nor did I have any desire to be there. I had been there when the Wall went up, and I was one of the first to drive through it. Of course, I couldn't have been happier that it was coming down, but I found myself wanting to press forward, not look back.

On the first Sunday after the Wall fell, Jan told me he was especially looking forward to attending church in East Berlin. Surely it would be a great time of rejoicing, of praise and gratitude to God for freedom restored—the freedom to worship, to teach the Bible, and to evangelize without fear of punishment. But when he arrived at the church, he was shocked to find it nearly empty.

Why? Because most of the members had gone to West Berlin to shop.

"They now go to the supermarket instead of coming to our Super-God who delivered us," the pastor lamented with a sigh.

As sad as it made me to hear this report from Jan, I do not blame or condemn those Christians. If I had lived in the shadows of East Berlin for all those years, I might have done the same thing. But their action served to remind me that capitalism is not a good alternative to communism if the King of glory is not invited.

◄o►

About every six weeks during that period of turbulence and triumph, our trucks delivered the New Testaments to distribution points in Russia, usually in shipments of one hundred thousand at a time. The final consignment arrived in early 1990. During the first week of March, I went back to Moscow to present the "last" New Testament to Patriarch Aleksi, the new head of the Russian Orthodox Church. I was accompanied by my colleague, Klaas, and a TV crew to document the event.

We returned to the Danilov Monastery for a lavish formal dinner, an evening reception with Patriarch Aleksi, and a closing ceremony in Aleksi's private chapel. He was a man of at least my age, with a long gray beard. He wore black vestments, a white headdress, and a large medallion on a chain around his neck. We both gave brief speeches, and then I presented Patriarch Aleksi the one millionth New Testament. I also gave him a copy of *God's Smuggler.*

"This is the last of the first one million," I said to him. "I hope I'll never have to smuggle Bibles into Russia again."

He nodded in agreement as he graciously accepted the books. Then he said, "Andrew, can we pray together?"

We went into his private chapel and stood before a wall of beautiful icons known as the iconostasis, which have for centuries been a part of the Russian Orthodox style of worship.

"Let us pray the Lord's Prayer together," he said, "you in Dutch and I in Russian."

As we prayed out loud, and I heard us both say "Our Father" in our own languages, it suddenly hit me: We Christians are all one family. In spite of this man's language and culture and appearance, his heart is just as hungry for the love of God as mine is.

We had the opportunity to visit several more churches during that visit. One was the Kuncevo Orthodox Church on the outskirts of Moscow. For many years it had been closed and used as a warehouse by the communists, and within the past year had been returned to the Orthodox church. Restoration would take at least five years, they told us, and the church would have to pay for it all.

At the end of the liturgy, during which people were lighting candles, singing, and kneeling on the ruined floors, the priest introduced us and handed out a few of our New Testaments to church members. Again the people pressed forward to receive a copy, and they expressed great gratitude to our team afterward.

I also visited a Baptist church in the midst of a similar restoration process. It was an absolute mess, and there was so much work to be done. Services were held upstairs while the sanctuary downstairs was being rebuilt. The good news, of course, was that the congregation had its church building back; but the bad news was that the high cost and huge amount of time required for the repairs hindered the other activities of the church.

One evening we attended a crowded service at the Moscow Baptist Church and spoke afterward with Nikolai Kolesnikov, one of the leaders there. With great enthusiasm he told me about dozens of requests they had received for Bibles—from schools and even from military academies. The church also regularly passed on Bibles to unregistered churches across Russia.

A personal highlight for me was meeting one of my heroes, Joseph Bondarenko, for the very first time in his own country. Known as "the Billy Graham of the Soviet Union," this courageous brother from Riga, Latvia, has devoted his life to evangelizing Russia. After enduring three prison terms of three years each, he had been released during the 1980s and was free to continue his work. For years I had followed his activity, and there I was with him on his own turf.

What a kind and gracious man he is, full of enthusiasm and love for the Lord. Together we went to Red Square to do interviews for our TV crew. Then Joseph started preaching to everyone in Russian and handing out New Testaments right in front of Lenin's mausoleum. One woman hardly knew anything about the Bible, so he explained the good news to her and asked her to read John 3:16 out loud. People listened eagerly and cried out to us for more Bibles. It was a moving scene.

When we had finished filming and talking to the people, we gave Joseph a box of seventy-eight Bibles to take to Siberia, where he was headed for three weeks of evangelistic meetings. Then we headed home to Holland.

◄○►

My involvement with the De Burght human-rights group continued during this period as well. In March of 1991 the group convened at the International Peace Palace in The Hague to arrange for the independence of the Baltic States. Joseph Bondarenko and his family visited me in Holland around that time, and I asked him what he thought about independence for his home country of Latvia.

Do you know what my brother said? "Andrew, I don't want my country to become independent because then I will lose my mission field." Put another way, if Latvia became an independent country, he probably would find it much harder to travel and evangelize in Russia.

His words astounded me. But they reminded me of an important truth for Christians: Nationalism can be a wonderful thing, but if our desire for political independence is greater than our desire to evangelize the world, we can never win against the forces of evil. The path of persecution may be the only way to victory—as it was for Joseph.

While Joseph was with us, he spoke at my home church and his whole family sang for us. I had never seen that church so crowded. The sermon he preached was so simple, and yet every word contained great authority.

As I listened to Joseph speak, a man sitting next to me leaned over and said, "Andrew, where does this man get his authority from?"

Without thinking I said, "Because he paid the price for it." And then, before I could catch myself, I added, "You and I *get* paid for it." Maybe I shouldn't have said it, but it's the truth.

After the sermon, I had a chance to sit and talk with Brother Joseph. I wanted to tell him about our seven-year prayer campaign for Russia, which had just recently ended. So much had happened during those seven years, during which we had prayed day and night. Not only Russia, but the whole world had been turned upside down, it seemed.

"Joseph," I said, "you know we prayed seven years for you."

He gently replied, "Andrew, please don't stop. We have also been praying—for the past seventy years."

I was back in my little corner where I belonged. Of *course*—they also prayed. They prayed for us. I had forgotten the very principle that I often preach about: *We need the suffering church as much as they need us.* We have as much to learn from them (perhaps even more!) as they do from us.

◄○►

Not even the defiant country of Albania could resist the changes sweeping over the communist world. In the late 1980s, our prayer teams who had walked through its cities and towns began to see answers to their prayers. The cruel tyrant Enver Hoxha, who had once said that in Albania "belief in God must be plucked out at its roots," had died in 1985, leaving a major crack in the country's tough exterior. Finally in 1990, his successor, President Ramiz Alia, started to relax some of the internal restrictions on its citizens.

There was no turning back after that. Soon the entire communist system fell apart, and many thousands fled the country. With no remaining natural resources and more than half the population unemployed, the situation degenerated into a state of near anarchy. Crime and corruption were rampant. Thieves would smash car windows and steal valuables while passengers were still in the vehicle. If the police came at all, they would either ask for a bribe or steal something else from the car.

At that point, a group known as Ancient World Outreach, in cooperation with a number of other missions including Open Doors, requested permission to conduct the first-ever evangelistic campaign in modern Albania. With the country in such dire need of spiritual revival, and the current movement in Europe toward free expression, we were not surprised to receive a yes answer.

What did surprise us, however, was how enthusiastic that yes answer was. Not only did they allow us to have our campaign, but they offered us the free use of the stadium in the capital city of Tirana. On July 1, 1991, the minister of culture, Prec Zogaj, officially opened the first meeting by saying, "There is a great need in Albania for this. The country needs spiritual matters."

I had the privilege of being the first of several preachers to address the crowd, which totaled eight thousand over a five-day period. Hungry for spiritual truth after decades of darkness, the people listened attentively in spite of the blustery weather. Albanian State Television broadcast the first service to the entire country, and the former Communist Party newspaper *Zeri i Populit* covered the event. Anticipation and interest were so great that a radio interviewer, after being told by one evangelist to keep his questions short because of time limitations, said, "No. I've been waiting ten years for this moment, so I'm going to take my time."

What an incredible week! On the final day we held a special meeting for 157 new converts and baptized 43 people in a nearby lake. During the campaign we were able to distribute ten thousand copies of the gospel of John, seven thousand New Testaments, and a great deal of other literature. Afterward we cooperated with European Christian Mission on a translation of the entire Bible in the modern Albanian language. Clearly the country was entering a new era.

The following year, at America's national prayer breakfast in Washington, D.C., I had some good conversations with a few of Albania's top political leaders who were attending for the first time. The Albanian ambassador to the United Nations came up to me afterward and said, "Brother Andrew, we must have this kind of thing in Albania, too." They were very enthusiastic.

An Albanian prayer breakfast never panned out, but later in the year several letters came to my office from the president and the prime minister. Would I please bring the Bible to Albania as soon as possible, the letters said, so that Jesus can speak in the Albanian language?

There were some curious expressions in letters of invitation. One was, "Could you come with the Bible so we can have a Bible party?" They didn't know what to call a Bible presentation ceremony. I actually liked the phrase "Bible party." They also wrote, "Please bring cheese and crackers and Coca-Cola for the Bible party."

I was very encouraged, and I pressed for completion of the Bible translation. At last in early 1993, it was finished and the first copies rolled off the press in May. By that time the war in Bosnia had begun, so we had to send our truck—loaded with the bulk of the Bibles plus plenty of cheese and crackers and Coke— through Italy and across the Adriatic Sea by ferry into Albania for the delivery. The next day we flew to Tirana with a small load of Bibles just in case the truck was delayed.

The event took place in the modern International Cultural Center, the very building that Hoxha had erected as a monument to himself. Originally there had been a mammoth statue of Hoxha chiseled out of a forty-two-ton block of marble, but I noticed it was gone.

"Whatever happened to that statue?" I asked the prime minister. "Is anything left of it?"

"No," he replied. "We totally ground it up into dust so that nobody could ever claim any piece of it." An interesting contrast to the destruction of the Berlin Wall, I thought, where pieces were not only collected but sold for profit.

There in that building, I stood to give Albania its first complete modern Bible. More than two hundred people attended the ceremony, including members of Parliament, the three secretaries of state for religion (representing Orthodox, Catholic, and Muslim adherents), and representatives from more than forty churches that had sprung up in recent years. A children's choir performed for the occasion.

After my brief address, several government leaders wanted to offer remarks. Zekri Palushi thanked us on behalf of the prime minister. "Our children don't have to believe in Enver Hoxha anymore," he said, "but may now learn to know the name of Jesus. This will enrich their spirits and minds."

Yili Vesjoe, the recently retired minister of education, added, "For many years we lacked this book. The Bible contains a message of peace, of love, and of a better life. After a period of dictatorship the people need a spiritual, moral, and economic revival. The Bible can contribute to this. The period of dictatorship has ruined the people, but the Bible can restore them."

Finally member of Parliament Pjeter Pepa reminded us of all the Albanians who had been killed for advocating the Scriptures: "The past fifty years, the devil reigned in our country. Now that we have the Bible, we hope the devil will be expelled."

When everyone had finished speaking, we all had ourselves one big Bible party.

◄○►

It was only a matter of time before the wave of freedom in Russia and Eastern Europe would affect our ministry at Open Doors. Since Bibles could be delivered and even printed legally in all the formerly communist countries, we no longer needed the skills of many of our personnel who planned and carried out our European smuggling operations. We ended up having to let go nearly half of our staff in Holland—thirty altogether—fine people who did fine work. So here in the office we experienced many mixed feelings. It was a time of sadness as we said good-bye to close friends with whom we'd worked for years, and yet it was also a time of rejoicing because we had reached one of the great milestones we'd all been working toward.

Our income also dropped significantly, apparently because many supporters mistakenly thought that the fall of Soviet communism meant that our job as a mission was done. Far from it! Much follow-up work has been needed in these countries, most of which are still quite unstable politically, economically, and spiritually.

It's important to remember that there is no quick jump from totalitarianism to democracy. The problems are far from over. I predict that these countries will take as long to restore a democratic way of life as they took to break it down. As Christians who want to see the church grow in these countries, we must be patient, but also alert. After all, if we are allowed in, so are the Muslims and the Buddhists and the Hindus.

For our part, in 1991 we followed up on the Target One Million Project in Russia with Project Samuel, in which we launched the delivery of a million children's Bibles. With so many other missions providing regular Bibles, our goal was to reach the little ones who had for generations been forbidden to hear Bible stories.

Now we are working primarily in the Central Asian republics where missions activity is minimal. As always, I want to do what nobody else is doing. Then when the doors open and others can freely get involved, we move on.

Communism, by the way, is certainly not dead yet. Ask anyone in China or Cuba or some African countries with a strong Marxist presence. The church still suffers in all of these countries, and we still have many workers taking Scriptures and support to the believers. But now that the the Iron Curtain has fallen, we are able to devote more of our resources and attention to a spiritual battle much greater than anything we experienced under communism. I am speaking of the battle between the Christian world and the Muslim world.

Step Nine

◄○►

Use your platform to proclaim God's message.

I will never forget the day in March of 1990 when I stood in Moscow's Red Square and watched Joseph Bondarenko preach the gospel openly in Russian. He was doing the very thing that had landed him in jail for nine years, but that time no one was stopping him.

Nor will I forget the time I looked out over the stadium of people in Tirana, Albania, and spoke in that country's first evangelistic campaign in many decades—with the full blessing of the government. In both cases I realized that that is what we strive for in Open Doors, and what all of us should strive for in our Christian lives: to proclaim the message of God openly and fearlessly. Of course, we don't just walk in and do it; we reach this point only after moving through the first eight steps and earning the right to speak.

Even after taking into account the fall of communism in the

Soviet Union and Eastern Europe, we still do not have the liberty to openly proclaim Jesus Christ in nearly half the world. Much of our work in Open Doors is still underground. But we always have the goal of breaking open the field so that we *can* proclaim. In any closed country or setting, we want to change the circumstances so that everyone can openly proclaim the lordship of Jesus.

To put it another way, freedom of religion is a fundamental human right, and we should press every government in the world to allow its citizens to exercise that right. Over the years various human rights organizations have brought international pressure to bear on countries that restrict the free expression of religion, with many positive results. In this book I have described the significant role of the De Burght human-rights group in restoring religious liberty to the countries of the former Soviet Union.

As Christians, we are concerned not only with the *right* to proclaim, but also with the proclamation itself. We seek to proclaim Jesus' lordship wherever human leaders or systems are worshiped—in other words, everywhere. Inevitably that will lead to a confrontation, as I mentioned in step five, because the gospel message *always* clashes with prevailing systems, whether political, economic, or even religious. In closed countries, our confrontation will likely be accompanied by persecution.

When we proclaim the lordship of Christ, the forces of evil around us leap into action, and the spiritual battle intensifies. Yet we need not be afraid. Why? Because we already know the outcome of the battle. It was decided two thousand years ago when Jesus died on the cross and rose from the dead. He has already defeated evil and death. And from the Scriptures we know that one day every knee will bow and every tongue confess that Jesus Christ is Lord (Philippians 2:10–11).

So the message we proclaim is one of victory through Christ. We win! Because we know what is going to happen, the rest and assurance we radiate will attract many people to hear our proclamation. But that means we must walk closely with God and stay grounded in his Word.

Remember the Old Testament story of Joseph? His proclamation began when he told Pharaoh that God was the one who gave him the interpretation of dreams. Then, after Pharaoh told him his two dreams, Joseph said, "God has revealed to Pharaoh what he is about to do" (Genesis 41:25). Now I love these words. They remind me of God's words just before he rained down judgment on Sodom and Gomorrah: "Shall I hide from Abraham what I am about to do?"

God is not hiding from us what he is going to do with this world. It is all written in Scripture, and it is our job to proclaim it to every person and every nation. In spite of the intense spiritual warfare—or perhaps *because* of it—I believe God will give us opportunities to proclaim the good news of Christ to people we never thought would be interested. Many of these people live in countries where the political system has toppled, or is about to topple. They have reached a point of deep dissatisfaction in their hearts. They may be more receptive to our proclamation than ever before.

Islam is very much a religion of proclamation. Five times a day, from millions of minarets around the world, the piercing call to prayer blasts over cities and towns. That adds up to billions of proclamations over Islam's 1,300-year history. During the Iran-Iraq War in the mid-1980s, I visited Iran to encourage the Christians there. At the airport in Tehran before returning home, I wanted to buy a few things that would remind me of Iran. I saw a cassette at the newsstand labeled *Koran,* and since I didn't own an audio copy, I thought I'd buy it.

"Is that the Koran?" I asked, immediately realizing I shouldn't have.

"Yes, I'll put it on," the man said, and without waiting for my answer he stuck it in the cassette deck and pressed the play button. Suddenly the whole airport was filled with the chanting of the Koran.

"Stop it! Stop it!" I said in desperation. I hated to be responsible for broadcasting the Koran throughout the Tehran airport. So I quickly bought the tape just to get it out of there. When I got home, I put it on my shelf and never played it again.

Christianity also depends heavily on proclamation. I think of Moses, who fearlessly stood up to Pharaoh and proclaimed, "Let my people go!" At the end of his life, when he wanted to sum up all the teaching he had received from God and given to his people, he put it in the form of a song, which is easier to remember than prose. "Now write down for yourselves this song and teach it to the Israelites and have them sing it," God told Moses. "And when many disasters and difficulties come upon them, this song will testify against them, because it will not be forgotten by their descendants" (Deuteronomy 31:19, 21). Later Moses recited the entire song in the hearing of all the Israelites.

So the next time we hear chanting from the mosque, or anyone reciting a mantra for that matter, remember that as Christians we have our own godly proclamations, and we can use them to pray against evil ones. I always make a point of instructing ex-Muslims to say, *Jesus is Lord, Jesus is Lord,* to themselves every time they hear the blaring of the mosques. That is a form of proclamation, even if it is not spoken out loud before a group of people. They are still proclaiming Christ to themselves and to the unseen powers.

Even reading the Bible out loud is a way of proclaiming (Revelation 1:3). But we must not be satisfied with that. We need to take the message we have proclaimed out of our bedrooms and living rooms and into our schools, workplaces, and neighborhoods. We must remember that this is still God's world, and we can claim it for him. We can allow every place where we put our feet to be one that we have claimed for the kingdom of Jesus Christ.

Many countries and peoples of the world still do not have the freedom to proclaim the gospel. They desperately need people like us to help them proclaim the will of God, the revelation of God, the power of God, the kingdom of God, the principles of God, the love of God, the righteousness of God, and the peace of God. One day they will all proclaim his name, and the Bible says that will be soon! So take courage, and joyfully proclaim the victory he has already won.

PRAYER

Lord, thank you that even though I'm in the midst of a spiritual battle, the victory is already yours. Help me to proclaim that victory today.
Amen.

Chapter Eleven

◄o►

The Muslim Challenge

*T*hough I've traveled periodically to the Middle East throughout my ministry and made many Christian friends, for years I remained naïve about the presence of the church in the strict Muslim countries. I had assumed that there simply was no church, that the Islamic fundamentalist governments had stamped it out of existence.

Imagine my surprise one day in the late 1970s when a Middle Eastern man came up to me at a conference and said, "Brother Andrew, when are you coming to visit the churches in Iran?"

He identified himself as an evangelical Iranian pastor, and he was serious.

Dumbstruck, I looked at Johan, who was standing next to me, and then I turned back to the man. "What do you mean by 'the churches in Iran'?" I said in amazement. "Is there really a church in that country?" Ayatollah Khomeini was in power, and his fanatical Islamic regime had condemned virtually anything that smelled Western, so I figured the Christian church was long gone.

Was I mistaken.

My colleague Johan and I finally went to Iran for the first time in the winter of 1981, at the height of Khomeini's power and in the middle of the Iran–Iraq War. Only a couple of months earlier the hostages had been released from the American embassy in Tehran.

Our plane had to land in the midst of a nasty snowstorm. Inside the terminal was total mayhem, with hundreds of people waiting for hours for their luggage, and everyone rushing madly to the baggage area when something did arrive. People were fighting, yelling, and cursing at each other in frustration. We eventually spotted our suitcases behind a row of desks, and after climbing over to reach them, we managed to pass through customs and out the door, where a car was waiting for us.

The chaotic atmosphere of the airport seemed to continue as we made our way to the Christian church. Most of the traffic lights didn't work, and people pretty much ignored the ones that did, causing traffic snarls and fender benders. Finally we reached the small church building, which was on the same street as the American embassy. It faced a large square and a huge mosque where at that time a million Muslims would show up for Friday morning prayers. We said to each other, "What would happen if a million Christians gathered each week to pray in Amsterdam or Washington, D.C.?"

Inside the church was a little bookshop where copies of *God's Smuggler,* recently published in the Farsi language, were displayed. I half expected the believers to complain about the economic, political, and spiritual mess the Ayatollah had brought upon the country. What I heard instead caught me by surprise.

"God has been good to us," they said. Because of all the chaos and confusion, the church had been able to use the same permit five times to print more Bibles. In addition, more Muslims had been coming to the church, and the believers had been able to share God's love with them, though they were not allowed to proselytize.

My Christian brothers went on to make another startling statement. "Khomeini has been the biggest blessing our country has ever had," they told me, "because he has revealed Islam for what it really is. Before he came, Islam was a pretty package all wrapped up on the mantelpiece. Khomeini took the parcel, undid the wrapping, and showed the world what is really inside."

Indeed, many I spoke with had personally experienced Islam's darker side in the form of intolerance, harassment, and frequent police surveillance and interrogation. Yet the persecution seemed only to strengthen their faith.

What a wake-up call that visit proved to be! After all the preaching I'd done about no country being closed in God's eyes, I realized I'd been writing off places such as Iran and Saudi Arabia, assuming that no church could possibly survive there. My eyes were opened, and I wanted to do something about it.

First we informed our prayer partners around the world and asked them to intercede for their brothers and sisters in Iran. Then during the 1980s we began to support small projects that would strengthen the church, such as supplying study materials and libraries for the pastors, and providing financial assistance to their families.

As we continued to pray for those church leaders, God gave us another idea. Why not bring some of them out of the country for a week of encouragement, teaching, and rest? Surely they could use a break from the daily pressure of life as Christian ministers in a society so hostile to their faith. So in 1991 we came up with a plan to fly twelve key pastors and their wives to a relatively free Middle Eastern country for a holiday.

All of the arrangements had to be made covertly so as not to attract the attention of the Iranian secret police. Even then, as Johan and I waited to pick them up at the airport near our retreat center, we had no idea how many of the couples would make it out of Iran. (Citizens of Iran are normally allowed to travel out of the country, but since the pastors were on the police's surveillance list, the chance of being followed or detained was much greater.) We worried a bit after learning the flight had been delayed, but when it finally arrived and the passengers came through the gate, I recognized a few of the pastors we had met earlier. We breathed a sigh of relief that at least *some* of them had made it.

One by one the couples came through customs. The wives were wearing head scarves even in the hot weather to comply with Iranian laws. They all remained fairly reserved at first since they were still in public, but I could see the excitement in their faces. Only one couple out of twelve was held up at customs, and we had to wait for forty-five minutes while they were thoroughly checked. Though they were out of Iran, they were still concerned that someone had been watching them on the plane.

When we finally climbed into our rented van and drove away from the airport, the couples immediately relaxed as if they had been holding their breath for the entire flight. The women yanked off their scarves and everyone laughed. It was almost like they had been released from prison.

We enjoyed a very special week togehter. To spend time with those wonderful, dedicated Christians was a tremendous privilege. In the mornings Johan and I offered teaching and encouragement from Scripture, and one Iranian pastor who lived in the West spoke to the group as well. There was time for worship, for fellowship, and for swimming or walking along the beach.

Over the course of the week several of the men shared how difficult it was to serve as a pastor under Islamic law—and yet how thrilling it was to see God at work in Iran. We heard more about Mehdi Dibaj, a pastor we had been praying for who had been imprisoned—though never formally charged—for the "crime" of converting from Islam to Christianity some forty years ago.

One minister in the group described how he was detained by the police, interrogated at great length, and then at midnight was locked in a hotel room in Tehran. After he had sat there for several hours, praying and wondering what would happen next, some of the interrogators came to his door. He tried to prepare himself for another round of grilling. But when they came into the room, their faces looked different.

"Tell us more about this Jesus you spoke of," they said to him. During the earlier interrogation he had told them about what Christ had done in his life. They wanted to know more. So he told them, and that very night they gave their lives to Jesus.

Another pastor shared how the Lord had protected them during the terrible earthquake in 1990. The whole area where they lived was destroyed—except for the church. At one point during the crisis, he said, he saw an angel holding up the roof of the church building.

It was hard to say good-bye at the end of the week, but I was happy that they were returning home refreshed and encouraged —and well-stocked with Scriptures and Christian literature.

Conditions worsened for the Iranian churches shortly after that conference. People were arrested, the Bible society office was closed down, and several key pastors left the country— though they continue to serve their brothers and sisters in Iran. One man who could have left but chose to stay was pastor Haik Hovsepian. I had first met his brother at the conference and later had the opportunity to meet Haik. He was a brave, dedicated leader who spoke out when the Iranian government tried to curb the activities and liberties of Christians. He had also been pressing for Pastor Dibaj's release.

In December 1993 I had the privilege of seeing Haik in Pakistan, where both of us were speaking at a pastors' conference. I was so impressed with the zeal of this brother and the challenges he set forth. It's one thing to lecture about persecution and suffering from a textbook; it's quite another to teach from personal experience. Having narrowly escaped death several times for his faith, Haik truly represented the suffering church in Iran. Though we spent only a short time together, I felt very close to him in spirit.

As we shook hands and bade each other farewell at the end of the seminar, he looked me straight in the eyes, gripped my hand firmly, and said, "Andrew, when they kill me, it will be for speaking, not for being silent."

When, not if.

Back in Iran, Haik continued to preach the gospel boldly. He also vigorously defended his Christian brother Mehdi Dibaj, who by then had spent nine years in jail. Pastor Dibaj was a remarkable man, completely dedicated to God and willing to die for him. For two of those nine years, Mehdi had been confined to a dark cell of only one square meter in size. Yet during that time he had grown so close to the Lord that when he was later transferred to a regular cell with other prisoners, he asked if he could be returned to his solitary cubicle. There, he said, he would not be ridiculed, and he would have uninterrupted time with God.

During the same month that I saw Haik, the Iranian government decided to formally charge Mehdi with the crime of apostasy, which carried the death sentence. He was allowed to defend his case in a court hearing, but he chose instead to present a deeply moving testimony of his faith in Jesus Christ. Here is a small portion of his "defense":

"They tell me 'Return!' [to the Muslim faith]. But from the arms of my God, to whom can I return? Is it right to accept what people are saying instead of obeying the Word of God? It is now forty-five years that I am walking with the God of miracles, and his kindness upon me is like a shadow. I owe him much for his fatherly love and concern.

"He is our Savior and he is the Son of God. To know him means to know eternal life. I, a useless sinner, have believed in his beloved person and all his words and miracles recorded in the gospels and I have committed my life into his hands. Life for me is an opportunity to serve him, and death is a better opportunity to be with Christ. Therefore I am not only satisfied to be in prison for the honor of his holy name, but am ready to give my life for the sake of Jesus my Lord and enter his kingdom sooner."

Unmoved, the court convicted him anyway and sentenced him to death by hanging. When the news reached us, we immediately alerted our prayer chains, and soon thousands of Christians around the world were interceding for Brother Dibaj. Pastor Haik, too, was praying—but he was also speaking out.

Barely three weeks later we received a wonderful answer to our prayers: Brother Dibaj had been released. Apparently the public outcry—combined with all those prayers—had caused the government to back down.

Little did we know, however, that the government had not abandoned its goal, but had merely changed its approach. Rather than go through the official court system, it would resort to unofficial means to do its dirty work.

Just days after Mehdi's release from prison, Haik disappeared while driving to the Tehran airport to pick up a friend. He was kidnapped and brutally murdered.

So in the midst of rejoicing over the miraculous release of Pastor Mehdi, we also mourned deeply for Pastor Haik. I especially felt the loss of this kindred spirit and courageous man of God.

At Haik's funeral, Mehdi said, "I should have died, not him. He had a wife and a family and a ministry." Mehdi once had a family as well, but while he was in jail, his wife had converted back to Islam and left him.

Haik's assassination was only the beginning. Five months later Mehdi Dibaj was killed as well, also under suspicious circumstances. Then Haik's successor, Tateos Michaelian, was shot in the back of the head. Three men of God slain within half a year. The government, of course, denied any involvement with the killings. The new leader of the church is keeping a low profile and works as part of a team to minimize their risks.

Since then, we have provided assistance to the families of these martyrs, and we are still working to strengthen the church in Iran by supplying them with God's Word and Christian literature. And we will continue to call upon the church worldwide to intercede on behalf of the church of Iran and especially its new leaders.

I have come to believe that Islam poses the biggest challenge to the church today. Not to political or economic systems, but to the church. Why? Quite simply, because we in the Western church don't come close to matching the level of commitment, determination, and strength of many Muslim groups. Christ and the Bible certainly call us to a radical commitment, but we don't show it in the way we live. Until we do, Islam will continue to be the world's fastest-growing religion—not because of its strength, but because of our weakness.

For that reason, I have devoted the rest of my ministry life to these two objectives: going to the Muslims in the name of Jesus, and doing my part to strengthen the church in the Muslim world. Really, it's the same thing I've always done, but because I'm focusing on a group that appears to be utterly closed to Christians, I feel as if I've embarked on a totally new career.

◄o►

One of the earliest prayers in the Bible is Abraham's prayer for his other son: "If only Ishmael might live under your blessing!" (Genesis 17:18). I believe that if more Christians will pray this prayer today, we will begin to have an impact for Jesus upon the world of Islam. That is why in 1991 we in Open Doors decided to launch another prayer campaign: ten years of prayer for the church in the Muslim world.

We're conducting it in a similar way to our campaign for the Soviet Union, but with two important differences. First, we are praying for ten years rather than seven because the Muslim world is much more closed to the gospel than the Soviet Union ever was. And second, we are focusing our prayers on the *church* in the Muslim world because it is much too weak and in some places virtually nonexistent. There was always a solid, active network of believers in Russia and Eastern Europe. Not so in the Arab countries.

There is another major obstacle to overcome if we are to reach out to the Muslims. We must forever set aside the idea that they are our enemies. We did this for decades with the Russians— they were the terrible, evil communists who were going to conquer the world. That very attitude on our part is why it took so long for their system to crumble. In our fear we did not go to them with the love of God.

Today many of us have created an enemy image of the Muslims. They are all terrorists who hijack our planes, blow up our embassies, and take innocent people hostage. Not only is this untrue, but the very minute we view them this way we make it impossible to reach them with the gospel. God cannot use us.

Several years ago I was interviewed for a Christian TV show in America, and I spoke about this tendency we have to create an enemy to focus on. Maybe it's because we find it easier to identify what we are *against* than what we are *for*. So I explained to the talk show host that the communists and the Muslims are not our enemies.

The interviewer was flabbergasted. He threw his hands in the air and said, "Well, Andrew, if these people aren't our enemies, then who is?"

"The devil," I told him, "but never people!"

On many occasions when we visited Christians in the communist countries, they told us that they had an easier life than we in the West. "We know who our enemy is," they would say, "but you do not." As long as we have an enemy image of any group of people, *we cannot love them.* God will not call us to any nation or people that we do not shed tears for when we pray for them.

We must also avoid taking sides politically in the various conflicts involving Muslims. We're easily tempted to label the "good guys" and the "bad guys," but anyone who has spent time studying the problems of the Middle East can tell you that every issue, every situation, is much more complex than it appears. Every side has both good and bad motives; every side has committed some good deeds and some atrocities. So instead of always looking for the enemy or taking a side, we should go to *all* sides with the love of Jesus. We should strive to be like the angel who met Joshua on the road as he was approaching Jericho (Joshua 5:13–14). Joshua asked him the same question we tend to ask: "Are you for us or for our enemies?" The angel replied, "Neither," and instead identified himself as part of the Lord's army.

I am not in any way a Muslim specialist, and I never will be. I keep reading and studying their philosophy and theology because I want to understand their needs, their hurts, their fears for the future and for eternity. Above all, I want to listen to them. Only then can I help.

—◄o►—

Every trip I've made to the Middle East, beginning with my earliest visits to Israel and Jordan in the mid-1960s, has been an education. More often than not it has been a *re*education because I've had to unlearn so many of the things I've been taught by Western church leaders. By being there, seeing the situation for myself, and talking with many people face to face, I've gained an entirely new perspective on this part of the world and its various peoples. Let me give a few examples.

• I learned that there are many Christians among the Palestinians. When I took time to speak with these fellow believers, they poured out their pain to me—specifically the pain of not being recognized by the Western church as part of the body of Christ. Many Christians in the West, they told me, are so obsessed with Israel and its place in biblical prophecy that they completely ignore the *church* in Israel, which today is 85 percent Arab. As a result, the believers there feel lonely, abandoned, betrayed.

In Gaza, a small Baptist church has been without a pastor for many years. Also, a desperately needed mission hospital there has a one-million-dollar deficit and is fighting for its survival.

Not only have Western Christians ignored the church in Israel, I was told, but they have also ignored the Israeli government's often inhumane treatment of the Palestinians. There always seems to be an outpouring of sympathy for Israel—and rightly so —when they are the victims of a terrorist attack, but Israel's acts of brutality toward the Palestinians tend to be excused or overlooked. Palestinian Christians sometimes get caught in this crossfire, but they have no one to stand up for them and support them.

• I learned that the percentage of Christians in the Middle East is shrinking at an alarming rate. For a variety of reasons, large numbers of them have emigrated during this century, and the trend continues. In Syria and Iraq, for instance, Christians at the turn of this century comprised between 30 and 40 percent of the population. Now that number is 3 or 4 percent. In Palestine and Jordan, the percentage of Christians dropped from 32 to 4 percent over the same period. In Israel, Christians make up only about 1.8 percent, according to Anglican bishops I spoke with.

The archbishop of Canterbury recently remarked that by the year 2000, Israel would be a "Christian Disneyland."

• I learned that just as Christians come in many varieties, so do Muslims. There are many Muslim groups and sects, and they disagree and fight with each other in much the same way that Catholics and Protestants have fought over the centuries. Some interpret the Muslim teaching of *jihad,* or holy war, to mean literal war and even terrorism, while others believe it simply means they should strive to obey koranic teachings. What I quickly came to realize was that Muslims were not a monolithic group of people who all believed and acted the same.

One thing I did notice, however, was that overall the Muslims exhibited a much higher level of commitment than that of most Christians I know. Especially among the fundamentalist groups, I have seen amazing dedication and zeal. A few weeks after the bus bombing in Tel Aviv, a leader of the radical group Hamas (who claimed responsibility for the act) praised the suicide bomber, who had proclaimed to the world, "Our love for death is greater than your love for life."

Television coverage of the Middle East conflict inevitably shows a scene of Muslim boys yelling and throwing rocks. What the reports don't mention is that the organized groups of these boys are carefully selected based on the strength of their religious commitment. Only those who lived by the words of the Koran, kept up with their prayers in the mosque, remained sexually pure, and used no drugs or alcohol would be allowed to participate. Further, before they were selected they had to express a wish to die for Allah, and prepare their parents for that possibility. One teenage boy, after hearing about the massacre of Muslims in a Hebron mosque, said, "If I knew another massacre would be taking place tomorrow, I would be sure to be there."

How can we as Christians match that kind of dedication? We can't. Or more accurately we *won't.* The Bible nowhere urges us to *seek out* opportunities to die, but it does say we need to be *willing* to die for the cause of Christ. Unfortunately many of us don't take our faith that seriously. And the Muslims know it.

• I learned that the church in the Middle East has not figured out how to handle Muslim converts. The problem is that in many Muslim countries, conversion to Christianity is illegal. Muslims who accept Christ can be dismissed from their families, can have their wives and children taken from them, can be sent to jail or even to their death. On the other hand, Christians and especially pastors in many Muslim countries can be arrested and jailed for evangelizing Muslims. Many of them simply discourage Muslims or Muslim converts from entering their church. As more and more Christian missions begin to reach out to the Muslim world, this matter of "convert care" will become a key issue.

• I have seen that there is a genuine openness to Jesus among some Muslim groups. The Koran considers Abraham, his sons, Moses, David, Solomon, and Jesus to be prophets, and it recognizes the Torah, the Psalms, and the Gospels as holy Scriptures—through the Koran is considered to be the last revelation. There are indeed opportunities for us to build bridges—if we are willing to go to them in love.

◄o►

Why have I spent so much time working among the Muslims? Because they are people for whom Christ died, just as he did for every one of us. As you know, I have always been concerned with reaching people most others aren't attempting to reach—and building up the Christians among them. That's why I naturally gravitate to groups such as the Palestinians.

In addition, I cannot stress strongly enough my sense of urgency that we reach out to as many Muslim and Arab groups as possible while they are still reachable because anyone who is reachable is also winnable. We've seen that there is a startling openness to the gospel among some of these people. But unless we go to them now in love and influence them in a Christian direction, the ongoing cycle of violence and revenge will force them to take hard-line, extremist positions. Then they will come to us—the "Christian" West—in judgment.

It is already happening, and we are still not doing anything about it. The World Trade Center bombing was only the beginning. On Dutch TV recently I saw a frightening documentary about the rise of militant Muslim activity in America. FBI spokesman Oliver Revell minced no words: "Hezbollah and the Hamas are very active in the United States. We now know that they have carried out military training operations including firearms practice, [and] the creation and construction of explosive devices and bombs."

I speak of this threat not to strike fear into our hearts, but to challenge the church of Christ to stand up and be the church. Unless we wake up and strengthen what remains, unless we live out our faith at least as seriously as the Muslims live theirs, unless we take the initiative and go to them before they come to us, within a few years we will be facing very dark days as Christians. That's why I am trying to seize every opportunity to reach out to the Muslims, wherever they are.

One incredible opportunity arose in my own backyard in Holland during the early 1980s. I got a phone call from the pastor of the American church in The Hague. He had been approached by a young Arab man who was looking for a Christian minister to pray with his sick father. The pastor wanted to know if I'd go with him to pray for the man.

Of course, I would. So together we went to a house in The Hague, and the son introduced us to his father, a tall thin fellow lying in bed. He was quite sick. As we talked with him, we learned that he was the former headmaster of a Christian school in Nazareth. We prayed with him for a while, had Communion, even sang a few hymns with him.

When it was time to leave, we went into the living room, where the son had been waiting. He was a big, muscular guy.

"So what do you do for a living?" I asked him, mostly to make conversation.

"I work for Chairman Arafat," he replied proudly. "I am his right-hand man." As it turned out, he was acting as the main West European "ambassador" for the PLO.

"Hmm, that's interesting," I said. "Can you get me through to your boss?"

No problem, he told me. One phone call would do it.

Returning home that day, I could hardly believe what had just transpired. I had come simply to pray for a sick man, and had left with a direct connection to PLO Chairman Yasir Arafat.

Since then, I've had the opportunity to visit with Mr. Arafat, give him a Bible, and talk about Jesus with him. It made me feel good when, shortly after I had met with him, I read an interview in an English newspaper in which he stated that he read in his Bible every day. (It just *might* have been the one I had given him —who knows!)

◄○►

During the mid- to late-1980s, I spent a great deal of time visiting war-torn Lebanon, encouraging the believers and attempting to build bridges between the various warring factions. With Bibles in hand, I went to see the prime minister and the president and most of the generals of the various armies engaged in civil war.

One very promising relationship began in early 1988 on a plane flight from Rome to Beirut. I noticed a distinguished man with a turban sitting in the front row of the first-class section, surrounded by bodyguards. Sensing that he was an important man, I began to pray for him and for the opportunity to speak with him. I also made a point of walking past his seat to the rest room four or five times and making eye contact.

He turned out to be the Grand Mufti—the spiritual leader of all Sunni Muslims in Lebanon. We chatted briefly, and I gave him a copy of *God's Smuggler*. He in turn invited me to visit him in his office. Perfect.

So the following week I showed up at the Grand Mufti's little palace, located in the center of East Beirut, the Muslim area of the city. I had barely stepped into his office when he said, "Andrew—that book you gave me. Every day after dinner I have been reading it at the table to my children."

We had a meaningful time of conversation and sharing about our hope for peace. I presented him with a Bible. Then he said, "Andrew, this Jesus of yours—we know him better than you do because he was one of us. He lived among us, he knew our culture, he spoke our language. And he felt our pain." When I left that day, I felt greatly encouraged by the possibility of further dialogue with this Muslim leader.

Six weeks later, he and all of his bodyguards were blown to bits by a car bomb.

What can a person do who lives where such acts of terrorism are commonplace? He can get out of there as fast as he can, as many do, or he can choose to stay and be a representative of Christ.

Lucien Accad, head of the Middle East Bible Society based in Beirut, is one of those courageous Christians who never left. He and his family live in a modest flat on a hill with a beautiful view of Beirut. During the worst period of the civil war, the flat was nearly destroyed several times by artillery shells crashing through the windows and into his living room.

The last time it happened, Lucien's family had gone down to the bomb shelter in the basement, where they were watching a video of *The Hiding Place*. He was making a phone call in the kitchen, behind the living room wall, when a shell scored a direct hit, knocking him to the floor and demolishing most of the flat. Because he had been standing behind that wall, his life was spared. The explosion left him deaf for a week or so, but other than that, he was not really hurt.

I went to see him shortly after that shelling, and we sat there amidst the rubble that was once his living room. He was understandably in low spirits, and he spoke of giving up and leaving the country altogether.

After spending a day with him there, I could see why. I felt like a yo-yo, dashing down to the basement with the family, where we would sing and read together until the shelling stopped, and then traipsing back up the stairs to what was left of the flat. The basement was roughly the size of one apartment, and it had to hold all the people from the building. There was no network television available, but a generator made it possible for them to watch movies on a VCR.

"Lucien," I finally said, "have you ever seen a spider spinning an elaborate web? When he finally finishes, it is a beautiful work of art. But what does the spider do if his web is destroyed? Within a minute he is busy spinning another web. That's what you've got to do now. You've got to rebuild."

Somehow he found the strength to pick up the pieces and start again. He still lives there today. I don't think he was encouraged so much by what I said as he was by my willingness to go there and simply be with him in that shelter.

◄○►

Though most of my recent travel has been in the Middle East, I have also visited other Muslim countries. Usually the body of believers I found was small and badly in need of encouragement, but very much alive. Inevitably the church leaders would tell me things I'd never heard before about how God is at work in their country.

The situation in Iran remains very tense, for example, and because of the rise of Muslim fundamentalism and radicalism and polarization, I believe it will only get worse. The devil is working hard to exterminate the church there right now. And the church is learning how to resist fear and grow in boldness and confidence. Maybe because of all the suffering the country has endured, Iran will be one of the first countries to reap the benefits of the gospel.

Pakistan is another country where Islamic law has become the law of the state. It began slowly several years ago, but more and more of the koranic justice system has taken effect each year until now restrictions are much fiercer. Fundamentalism is working its way into every aspect of society, and the strict Islamic laws are overtly discriminatory against Christians.

Take the case of Pakistani Christian Gul Masih, for instance, who was imprisoned in Pakistan on trumped-up charges of "blaspheming the Prophet." Or that of twelve-year-old Salamat Masih (no relation), who was convicted of scribbling blasphemies on the wall of the mosque—even though he could neither read nor write. Both were sentenced to death, but by the grace of God and a massive letter-writing effort on the part of Open Doors supporters and many other ministries and individuals, they were eventually released. But not every story has a happy ending.

—◄o►—

In this chapter I've hardly scratched the surface in explaining the needs of the church in the Muslim world. Nor have I talked about Muslim countries such as Egypt and Indonesia where there is a tremendous reservoir of Christians. The Coptic Orthodox Church in Egypt, founded by the apostle Mark, is nearly two thousand years old and seven million strong. There are many born-again believers among them. And among the many islands of Indonesia, explosive church growth over the past thirty years has swelled the number of evangelical believers to more than thirteen million.

It is in countries such as these, where the church is successfully operating amid a majority Muslim population, that Christians should take the lead in reaching out to the Muslims. They've lived and worked side by side with them long enough to know their needs, their hurts, their fears, and their deep spiritual hunger. They know the language and the culture. They are better able to build bridges and share the love of Christ than any missionary group. That's why we've focused our ten-year prayer campaign on the *church* in the Muslim world.

The truth is, we all need to come to grips with the rise of Islam —in Asia, in Europe, in Africa, even in the United States. Its strength and influence will most surely increase in the years to come. And the only way we in the church will be able to stand firm is to wake up, listen for the calling of God today, wherever we are, and then take that call seriously.

A recent experience I had at the Israeli airport in Tel Aviv symbolized both the problem in the world today and the solution that can be found only in Christ.

Airport security is (understandably) very tight there, and every passenger is interviewed by one, two, sometimes three agents before being allowed on the plane. They want to know where in Israel you traveled and what you were doing there. If you have visited any places that are known to be areas of unrest or anti-Israeli activity, you will be detained and grilled further, sometimes for hours. Every square inch of your luggage is inspected. If you miss your plane, tough luck—you'll just have to book another flight.

Since I tend to *avoid* the safe areas and tourist spots, passing through the airport "gauntlet" has been a grueling experience for me on several occasions. Once I had to strip off nearly all my clothes and stand in a separate inspection booth. It was so embarrassing.

On this particular trip, two friends had brought me to the airport. I realized I had visited the same places as before, and I prayed that I wouldn't have to endure another long interrogation: *Lord, I'll do anything for you if you will please save me from this humiliation. It takes so long and I am so tired. I don't think I can stand it.*

As I stepped out of the car, one of my friends said, "Andrew, when you get to the security check, try to get a man and not a woman inspector—the women are much more fanatical."

Guess who I got?

"So where have you been?" the uniformed woman said sternly.

I sighed and handed her my passport. Usually when I go to Israel, I obtain a new passport in Holland so it is not loaded with stamps from the "wrong" countries. This trip I hadn't been able to arrange for one in time. The pages seemed to shout at her, Lebanon! Egypt! Saudi Arabia! Plus, my suitcase was full of stickers and tags from other "forbidden" airports.

"I have been in Bethlehem," I said, knowing she wouldn't be happy about it. Bethlehem is in the West Bank, Palestinian territory occupied by Israel.

"Where else."

"Kiryiat Arba."

Her eyes flashed in disbelief. "What were you doing there?" she demanded. Kiryiat Arba is a very rightest Jewish settlement, and because of the unrest, a curfew had been imposed that week in nearby Hebron.

"Well," I said, "the son of a Dutch friend of mine lives there with his family, and he was recently shot by a Palestinian terrorist. I wanted to console the family."

The inspector appeared to soften a bit. "Bethlehem one day and Kiryiat Arba the next—that is quite a change in location, sir."

"Yes," I said, "but they are both about people who suffer." Not a vast, faceless ethnic group to project our hatred upon, not a new enemy to replace the communists, but children of Abraham, people created in the image of God, people in need of a Savior whose name is Jesus.

I looked at her and saw tears in her eyes. She closed my passport with all the wrong stamps in it and waved me through. Shortly thereafter I boarded my flight for home.

Step Ten

Allow God's power to flow through you into a needy world.

Sometime in the late 1980s I spoke with a young American missionary in Cyprus about the needs in the Middle East.

"What is the answer to all this conflict?" I asked him.

"Power evangelism," he replied.

My heart sank—not because I don't believe in power evangelism, the term coined by some Christians to refer to miraculous accompaniments to evangelism, but because real power evangelism requires more. By power evangelism I mean the power of God in the life of a man or woman who is totally dependent on him. It is not the starting point, but the result, the culmination, of years of planning, prayer, preparation, presence, and so on. And it is not so much something we possess or achieve as something we *reflect*—others see the power of God demonstrated through us.

I am going to take one last look at the account of Joseph

because his incredible life truly embodied all ten steps. After Joseph proclaimed God's truth to Pharaoh and interpreted his dreams, Pharaoh responded with an amazing statement: "Can we find anyone like this man, one in whom is the spirit of God? . . . Since God has made all this known to you, there is no one so discerning and wise as you" (Genesis 41:38–39).

Pharaoh recognized the power of God in Joseph. (His words take on even greater significance when we consider that pharaohs were themselves acknowledged as gods while in office.) And because he saw that divine power, he then bestowed upon Joseph earthly power over all Egypt, second only to Pharaoh himself. He gave Joseph his signet ring, dressed him in fine robes, put a gold chain around his neck, gave him a choice chariot, and even presented him with his daughter as a wife (41:40–45).

As Christians following the steps I have outlined in this book, we should concern ourselves not so much with the offices or the trappings of power, but instead with the *stewardship* of power and the *influence* we can be for God's greater purposes. Somewhere along the line Joseph realized that God had brought him to Egypt for a special purpose—to preserve life (Genesis 45:5). I'm sure he didn't know at first what that purpose was or how it would be achieved. But as he faithfully followed God, seizing opportunities to share about him with others and in effect moving through the steps I've described in this book, God's purpose became more and more clear to him. Where are the Josephs in the courts of today's world?

It is the realization that God is using us as part of a plan much greater than our lives that moves us into the power stage of evangelism. Of course, God's plan for us is *always* bigger than our lives. But when we finally take hold of that purpose, experience God's power, and allow ourselves to be used to preserve life or build up the church or influence the policies of a corporation or a country, then we will have truly accepted his charge over our lives.

How will we feel in this "power" stage of evangelism? We will probably experience a sense of smallness, of inadequacy, of relying completely on God's power because we have none of our own. That is exactly as it should be, and it is the only way in which we will be truly effective. And because the situation we were first called to has now changed, we are brought back to step one, where we listen for God's prophetic word all over again. He may be calling us to a new situation or to a different aspect of our current one. But we will now have a fresh opportunity to travel through these steps with deeper faith and confidence.

PRAYER

Lord, help me to surrender to your power
and your greater purpose for my life.
Amen.

Appendix A

Ten P's — Ten Prayers

concept	step	my daily prayer
1. Prophetic	Listen to God's prophetic Word for today.	*Lord, cause me to hear your prophetic Word for my life today. And lead me to the places and people who need to receive that Word— even at the risk of being thought a fool.*
2. Planning	Plan to do today what Scripture says.	*Lord, help me to accept your prophetic Word today and plan my life based on it. Allow me to take the initiative in advancing your kingdom, and keep that initiative even in enemy territory.*
3. Prayer	Become persistent in prayer.	*Lord, as I plan my life of service to you, I pray **for** the working out of your will in my situation and I pray **against** every evil force that opposes your will.*
4. Preparation	Prepare to live as a Christian full time.	*Lord, make me the proper tool in your hand. Cause me to grow in my relationship with you so that when opportunities arise to reap your harvest, I will be completely prepared.*

5. Penetration	Penetrate every devil-inspired boundary or barrier.	*Lord, help me to do something for you today that I have never done before.*
6. Presence	Maximize your opportunities by being present.	*Lord, show me how I can bring your presence to the places it is needed most, simply by being there myself.*
7. Profile	Establish your profile as a Christian.	*Lord, help me to live in such a way that your presence in my life is seen by others. Make me to be a blessing to someone today.*
8. Permanence	Become part of a permanent presence wherever you are.	*Lord, you have called me for a purpose. Wherever you lead me, help me to stay there and serve you faithfully.*
9. Proclamation	Use your platform to proclaim God's message.	*Lord, thank you that even though I'm in the midst of a spiritual battle, the victory is already yours. Help me to proclaim that victory today.*
10. Power	Allow God's power to flow through you into a needy world.	*Lord, help me to surrender to your power and your greater purpose for my life.*

Appendix B

Open Doors International Vision Statement

We believe that all doors are open and that God enables his body to go into all the world and preach the gospel. We therefore define our ministry as follows:

• *To strengthen the body of Christ living under restriction or persecution by providing and delivering Bibles, materials, training and other helps, and encouraging it to become involved in world evangelism.*

• *To train and encourage the body of Christ in threatened or unstable areas, to prepare believers to face persecution and suffering, and to equip them to maintain a witness to the gospel of Christ.*

• *To motivate, mobilize, and educate the church in the free world to identify with and become more involved in assisting the suffering church, believing that when "one member suffers, all the members suffer with it" (1 Corinthians 12:26 NKJV).*

How You and Your Church Can Make a Difference

Prayer—The believers in persecuted lands live in a fierce spiritual battlefield. They need focused, intercessory prayer. Open Doors will send a special "Prayer Force Alert" to all those interested in praying for these dear brothers and sisters.

Bible Couriers—For decades, Open Doors has been helping believers carry Bibles and Bible study aids into the areas of greatest persecution. God uses ordinary people to take his Word to people living where faith costs the most. You can be one of them.

Adult and Children's Bibles—Many persecuted believers have been beaten and imprisoned for their faith, yet don't have a Bible of their own. The young people in persecuted lands are special targets for false teaching and government control. Leaders know that they must have control of the minds of the youth if they are to stop the spread of Christianity. Open Doors is providing the church with special adult and children's Bibles that present the truth through words and pictures. Your generous gifts make this possible.

Leader Training for Church Growth and Evangelism—Most church leaders in persecuted lands have never had any formal training. Seminaries either don't exist or have been destroyed. Open Doors provides special leader training tailored to the needs and culture of each area. You can help sponsor the training and Christian library materials for one or more brave leaders.

For more information, write:

Open Doors
PO Box 53
Seaforth
New South Wales 2092
AUSTRALIA

Open Doors
PO Box 597
Streetsville
Ontario L5M 2C1
CANADA

Portas Abertas
CP 45 371
CEP 04010-970
Sao Paulo
BRAZIL

Portes Ouvertes
BP 5
F-67036 Strasburg
Cédex
FRANCE

Porte Aperte
CP 45
37063 Isola della Scala
Verona
ITALY

Open Doors
PO Box 47
3850 AA Ermelo
THE NETHERLANDS

Open Doors
Box 6123
Auckland 1
NEW ZEALAND

Åpne Dorer
4602 Kristiansand
NORWAY

Open Doors
PO Box 1573-1155
QCCPO Main
1100 Quezon City
PHILIPPINES

Open Doors
1 Sophia Road
03-28 Peace Centre
SINGAPORE 0922

Geopende Deure
Box 990099
Kibler Park 2053
Johannesburg
SOUTH AFRICA

Open Doors
Shehwa Officetel 406
Karakdong 79-4
Songpa-Gu
Seoul 160
SOUTH KOREA

Portes Ouvertes
Case Postale 267
CH-1008 Prilly
Lausanne
SWITZERLAND

Open Doors
PO Box 6
Witney
Oxon OX8 7SP
UNITED KINGDOM

Open Doors
PO Box 27001
Santa Ana, CA 92799
USA